CANADA
AND THE
IRISH QUESTION

1867-PRESENT

CANADA AND THE IRISH QUESTION

1867-PRESENT

PHILIP JAMES CURRIE

Canadian Cataloguing in Publication Data

Currie, Philip James, 1963-
        Canada and the Irish Question, 1867-Present

Includes bibliographical references.
ISBN 0-9688275-0-0

    1. Irish question. 2. Canada-Relations-Ireland.
3. Ireland-Relations-Canada. 4. Ireland-Politics
and government-20th century. 5. Ireland-Politics
and government-1837-1901. 6. Irish Canadians-
History. 1. Title.

DA959.C87 2000   941.5082   C00-901714-3

Cover concept and design by Christine D. Currie
Cover Graphics by Shannon Erskine

Printed in Korea

For Christine

with love and gratitude

CONTENTS

INTRODUCTION

On Good Friday, 11 April 1998, an historic peace settlement was concluded by the key representatives of Irish nationalism and Ulster unionism at Belfast, Northern Ireland. Most observers hoped that the Good Friday Agreement, which had extracted significant compromises from a majority of Ulster's interested parties, would provide the basis for a peaceful future for the troubled province. For thirty years unionists and nationalists had been caught in a vicious cycle of violence and mutual distrust. Now the major players, including the major republican and loyalist paramilitaries, had agreed to disagree, to live and let live. It was a political document of historic importance that not only ushered in a more civil mode of discourse within Northern Ireland, but promised to redefine Anglo-Irish relations in an era of European integration.

Hosting the talks that led to the Agreement were Tony Blair, the British premier, and Bertie Ahern, his Irish counterpart. *Chairing* the talks, however, were three foreigners. They were George Mitchell of the United States, General John de Chastelain of Canada, and a former premier of Finland. It is not surprising that once external input was requested, a Canadian and American would become deeply involved in the process. Unlike Finland, Canada and the United States have received large numbers of Irish immigrants over the centuries, and many of their most prominent persons in politics, business, and religion have been of Irish extraction. Both countries, moreover, have long histories of involvement in Ireland's political affairs.

Without doubt, American involvement in Irish affairs is the better known. Influential elements within that country, a republic that secured its own independence from Great Britain by means of armed insurrection, have been interested in securing a similar separation for Ireland. American political culture, and the influence of the Irish Catholic vote in the United States, also ensured a significant amount of political support for Irish republicanism in Ireland. Canada's involvement in Irish political affairs, however, has been profoundly different. And, while significant, it has gone largely unwritten, and remains virtually unknown. This book will address this lamentable gap in our knowledge of Canada's past.

Perhaps the single most significant factor directing Canadians' approaches to the Irish Question has been the fact that, unlike the United States, Canada does not possess a revolutionary heritage. It had no revolution and fought no civil war. And while everyone knows that Canada is an independent country, few agree on when this actually occurred. Canadians secured their independence from Great Britain gradually, and their country continues to hold a prominent position within the British Commonwealth of Nations. To this day Queen Elizabeth remains as Canada's head of state, and Canadian cities are dotted with statues of Queen Victoria and monuments to Canadians who fought and died in British wars. This evolutionary political culture has been a major factor in moulding Canadian approaches to the Irish Question, and in ensuring that they departed significantly from those of the United States.

Canadian approaches were also conditioned by the fact that, unlike the United States, Irish emigrants to British North America after 1800 were mostly of Protestant extraction and brought with them not Fenianism but the Orange Lodge. Canadians were further alienated from Irish republicanism by the armed Fenian incursions into Canada from the United States between 1866 and 1870. Militant Irish nationalism, therefore, quickly came to be associated not only with disloyalty to Great Britain, but questionable loyalty to Canada. Indeed, it was partly in reaction to Fenian activities on both sides of the Atlantic that Canadians first turned their eyes to Ireland. When, in the wake of the failed Fenian rebellion of 1867, Irish nationalists attempted to secure a measure of devolved government for Ireland within a British constitutional framework, considerable support was found for it in Canada. In fact the 'Canadian precedent' of limited self-government within the empire was embraced by many as a reasonable compromise between the *status quo* and an Irish republic. In the Canadian House of Commons resolutions of support were passed in support of Irish Home Rule on three separate occasions--1882, 1886, and 1903. After all, was it not the measure of self-rule enjoyed by Canadians that kept them loyal and contented? Indeed, when southern Ireland was eventually granted a measure of independence in 1921 its constitutional status, as outlined in the Anglo-Irish Treaty, was identical to that of Canada. Between 1922 and 1949 southern Ireland, variously known as the Irish Free State and *Eire*, existed, however uneasily, as a British dominion on the Canadian model.

The other political tradition that secured considerable support in Canada was Irish unionism, or loyalism. Its support derived from, among other things, an awareness that Ireland was not Canada. History, religion, geography, and a host of other factors, made Ireland's situation distinct not only from Canada's, but from all other British dominions. Geography, it was argued, dictated that the political and military indivisibility of the British Isles must remain a cornerstone of British defence policy. There was also the reality of Ireland's republican tradition, and its many influential supporters in the United States. Would this element accept Home Rule as a satisfactory solution to the national question? Many Canadians didn't think so. The Home Rule movement, therefore, was frequently dismissed as the Machiavellian vanguard of American-style Fenianism. The constitutional *status quo* was the unionist alternative. If Scotland, England and Wales were content to remain within the United Kingdom, why was Ireland so determined to break from it? Many Canadians who opposed Irish separatism in any form nevertheless conceded that the answer lay, at least in part, in Ireland's history of social and economic mismanagement under English rule. But the history of the larger British island suggested that such mismanagement was not inevitable. The answer to Ireland's woes, therefore, was benevolent government, not political separatism. This option alone would reconcile Ireland's desire for representative government with Britain's vital security needs. It will be seen that, although the pro-Union movement was initially slow to get organised, by 1912, the year of the third Home Rule bill, it was setting the agenda in Canada.

Neither the pro-Home Rule nor pro-Union faction in Canada would, however, see their vision for Ireland materialize. By the close of the Great War in 1918 moderate nationalism in Ireland had been replaced by militant republicanism. And by the time that southern Ireland became the Irish Free State--a British dominion based on the Canadian model--most of Ireland was voting for Sinn Fein, the political arm of the Irish Republican Army. Dominion Home Rule was accepted by Irish nationalists as a temporary stop on the road to a republic, not as an end in itself. In 1937 the Free State abolished the oath of allegiance and the post of governor-general. Between 1939 and 1945 it remained neutral in the war against Hitler to emphasise its independence, and in 1949 proclaimed itself a republic and left the commonwealth. Southern Ireland clearly preferred to enter the future as an American-style republic rather than a Canadian-style dominion. Oddly enough, however, the Irish prime minister of the day chose to announce his republican intentions while on a visit to Ottawa.

A HOUSE DIVIDED

This book will examine the political and cultural factors affecting Canadian interest in Irish politics since confederation. It will present the leading personalities and organisations involved in advancing the nationalist and unionist causes in Canada. What was the nature of Irish nationalism's appeal in Canada? Who were its main advocates and opponents? What accounted for its appeal, and for its demise? These, and many other questions, will be addressed in this book. Most importantly, it will show that the Irish Question in Canada was about a good deal more than Ireland. It was about Canada itself. It was about Canadian identity, Canadian principles, and the making of Canadian careers. It was about the nature of the empire to which Canada belonged, and the relationships between English and French in Canada, and between Catholic and Protestant. It was about Canadians' notions of their country's place in the world, and their notions of government.

It will also be seen that, throughout the years under examination, the Irish Question in Canada was fuelled by numerous factors tied to particular eras. When those factors were transformed by the years the nature of Canadian interest also changed. Despite the violence afflicting Northern Ireland since 1969--perhaps the longest period of political unrest in Irish history--Canadians have, for most of this time, remained emotionally detached. While Irish Americans have been actively involved in the conflict, and American politicians have exploited this to their political advantage, Canadians, Irish Canadians included, have remained largely detached, even disinterested in Irish affairs. The Canada that General de Chastelain is representing in Belfast is a radically different country from that of 1886, or 1912, or even 1969. While Ireland returned to fight yesterday's battles, Canada had moved on.

PART ONE

--CHAPTER ONE--

HOME RULE

> Never have I known an occasion when a parliamentary event so rang through the world as the introduction of this Bill. From public meetings and from the highest authorities in the Colonies...I receive the conclusive assurance that kindred people regard it with warm and fraternal sympathy. Our present effort is to settle, on an adequate scale, and once for all, the long-vexed and troubled relations between England and Ireland, which exhibit to us the one and only conspicuous failure of our race.[1]

In 1870 the Home Government Federation of Great Britain was founded in Dublin by Isaac Butt, an Anglo-Irish barrister convinced of the inequity of the existing Union between Great Britain and Ireland. Under the Union, Butt argued, a host of factors--geographic, political, religious, and economic--had determined that Ireland was, and must remain, the most distressed corner of the realm. The remedy for this situation, he had insisted, was the establishment of a parliament in Dublin with authority to legislate for all purely Irish affairs. Such a parliament would tackle Ireland's many problems, notably urban poverty and agrarian unrest, more competently than would half-interested and half-comprehending bureaucrats in London. Such a scheme would also provide an essential avenue for the expression of Irish identity and esteem, while keeping Ireland within a British constitutional framework. The Home Rule Federation, as it soon became known, received a rousing welcome in Ireland, and in the British general election of 1874 fifty-nine out of one hundred and five Irish candidates elected to the British House of Commons called themselves neither Liberals nor Conservatives--but Home Rulers!

3

Despite the persistent use of parliamentary obstructionism under the leadership of Butt's successor, Charles Parnell, the cause of Home Rule gained little ground before William Gladstone, former prime minister and leader of the British Liberal Party, announced his own conversion to Home Rule in 1885. In 1886 Gladstone managed to form his third government with Irish support, and, having previously stated his support for an Irish legislature, announced that a bill would soon be brought before the Commons. Gladstone's proposed legislation was undoubtedly a limited package that, while offering Irish nationalists the crux of their demands, would have kept authority for all imperial concerns--trade, taxation, diplomacy and war--firmly in the hands of the British government. The Royal Irish Constabulary would also be kept under federal authority for an unspecified period of time, and, like the imperial parliament itself, the Irish legislature would be divided into two Houses, with the Upper House maintaining the right of veto. Despite the limits inherent to the bill it was enthusiastically embraced by the Irish Party and its supporters.

Vociferous support for Gladstone's initiative also echoed from distant corners of the empire, not least from Canada. Those who professed their support for the principles underpinning the Irish bill included, not surprisingly, Canada's Irish community, and the Roman Catholic Church, which was, outside the province of Quebec, essentially an Irish church. But support for Home Rule in Canada was in no sense restricted to Irish Catholics. Not only did the provincial legislatures of Ontario and Quebec vote to send resolutions of support to Gladstone, but the Irish cause was vigorously advocated in the Canadian House of Commons. As early as 1882, three years before Gladstone's own conversion to the cause, that body had sent a communication to London offering its support for a measure of devolution for Ireland. Such support was motivated by any number of factors. Certainly one of the most important was the electoral clout of Canada's Irish Catholics. Another was a conviction that fundamental similarities existed between the

Canadian experience and that of the United Kingdom. Put simply, if 'Home Rule' worked in Canada, with its own entrenched ethnic and religious divisions, there was no reason why it should fail in the United Kingdom. How, it was argued, could anyone justify the granting of Home Rule to one corner of the empire and yet deny it to another? And, given its history of misrule at the hands of England, what corner of the empire deserved Home Rule more than Ireland?

Noone was more persistent in his advocacy of a measure of devolution for Ireland than Edward Blake, ex-premier of Ontario and current leader of the Official Opposition in the Canadian House of Commons. As a Canadian, and citizen of the empire to which Ireland belonged, he insisted that he had a legitimate interest--as had all Canadians--in the debate's outcome. And as an observer of the efficacy of Home Rule structures in reconciling alienated subjects to the British empire, he could only give Irish Home Rule his full support. As for the alienation of Ireland's Catholic majority, Blake insisted that it was the result of centuries of injustice meted out by Anglo-Protestant overlords. If French Canadians had legitimate grievances, and had entertained a legitimate demand for a measure of provincial autonomy, it paled in comparison to that of the Irish. Three consistent factors in England's involvement in Ireland over several hundred years, Blake insisted, were brutality, bigotry, and administrative stupidity. But, most damning, he insisted that it was not necessary to go back beyond the turn of the century to legitimise the call for Home Rule. "It is not needful here," he stated in the House of Commons, "to refer in detail to the more ancient events in connection with Irish history." No advocate of Irish Home Rule need refer "to the history of the conquest, to the history of the confiscations, to the history of the proscriptions, to the history of the penal laws..."[2] These were part and parcel of Britain's unhappy legacy in Ireland, but the need for Home Rule could be firmly proved by an examination of the previous eighty years alone-- beginning with the Act of Union itself.

   For little more than eighty years, he noted, Ireland had been managed by the parliament of the United Kingdom "..and I do not hesitate to say that the result of that management has been a dreadful failure." There had been time enough to try the question out. "Eighty years in the history of a country, and such eighty years as Ireland has experienced, is surely enough to try the question out."[3] Poverty, famine and widespread discontent were the Union's legacy. If Ireland was happy and well governed would more that one million of its sons and daughters have fled their homes in a desperate effort to reach the New World? No, Ireland was badly governed, and badly governed because it was not governed by Irishmen. It was governed by people of a different class, a different religion, and a different nationality. This Home Rule would remedy. It would also remedy the many evils of distant government by placing the seat of government in the Irish capital. The unionist experiment had failed, and responsible politicians, without reference to party or creed, must acknowledge this and embrace change.[4]

   The second point that Blake consistently emphasised was the Canadian precedent of Home Rule as a solution in Ireland. "[W]e are federalists ourselves," he reminded his colleagues in the House of Commons. "We are experienced in the benefits of Home Rule. If any people, in the wide world can speak of the difficulties engendered from the want of Home Rule, and the benefits to be secured by the grant of Home Rule, it is the people in whose name and in whose interests we sit and deliberate in this hall this night."[5] Canada, like the British Isles, was comprised of peoples of different races and creeds. If Home Rule worked here, why ought it not to work in the United Kingdom? Great Britain had given to Canada so much of its constitutional inheritance, an inheritance based on centuries of experience and compiled wisdom. Now Canada, much younger in years but quickly approaching adulthood, was in the position to repay the Mother Country with the wisdom attained by its experience.[6]

   Blake's third point was that Home Rule for Ireland was in the best interests of the British empire. What made enlightened thinkers so proud of the British empire was that it stood for liberty and fair play. This is what made Britain great. But if the British empire was to stand for democracy and fair play then Home Rule for Ireland could not be denied. And if the governors of that empire were concerned about Irish discontent, to deny Ireland Home Rule could only aggravate existing grievances. Was it not Home Rule that had turned Canada's Irish Catholic population into loyal citizens? Home Rule would usher in such a transformation of public sentiment in Ireland that it would be forever reconciled to the empire. No longer would England have to fear that Irish discontent would play into the hands of England's enemies. That discontent would have evaporated, being replaced by gratitude and contentment.[7]

For Blake, Home Rule was a settlement in which noone lost, with the possible exception of a few unrepresentative vested interests. Minutes into his speech in the House of Commons Blake was quoting Gladstone's evaluation of those who opposed Home Rule.

> Watching from day to day the movement of the currents of opinion during the present conflict, more and more I find it vital to observe the point at which the dividing lines are drawn on the side adverse to the Government. They are found, as I sorrowfully admit, in profuse abundance, in station, title, wealth, social influence, and the professions, and the large majority of them in the world, spirit and power of class. These are the main body of the opposing host.[8]

AGAINST HOME RULE: GOLDWIN SMITH

Not everyone was pleased with Blake's analogy, however, or with the messages of encouragement being sent back to England. Although slower to mobilise than the supporters of Home Rule, critics of Gladstone's Irish initiative soon began to express their own concerns in the press, parliament, and the streets. Noone was more persistent in his opposition to Home Rule, however, than Goldwin Smith, writer, publisher, and former Oxford professor. While not indifferent to Irish hardship, he insisted that Ireland's historic misfortunes, and England's long involvement in that country, must be understood within the larger context of European history--*not simply Irish history*. Given the geo-political realities in western Europe, at least since the 16th century, Ireland's proximity to England, and the smaller island's continued adherence to Roman Catholicism, its subordinate status within the British Isles was unfortunate but inevitable. These same factors had ensured that Ireland's economy would be intertwined with that of the larger island, and that the military indivisibility of the British Isles would be an unalterable pillar of British defence policy. While agreeing with Blake that British policy in Ireland had often been brutal, he admonished him to recall that the past had been a brutal era from which no people or society emerged unscathed. And given the many long-term factors involved in Ireland's ills, to blame British statesmen for every Irish ailment was ahistorical in the extreme.

He also insisted that the Irish Question was essentially an economic question, not, as Blake would have it, a political one, and as such Ireland was considerably better off remaining within a reformist United Kingdom. He repeatedly went to pains to point out that great social, economic and religious reforms had eventually followed the Union of 1800.[9] The removal of restrictions on Irish trade, Catholic Emancipation, the disestablishment of the (Protestant) Church of Ireland, land reform and a host of other initiatives had all been of immeasurable benefit to Ireland. Only the intentional misrepresentation of the facts, he insisted, continued to sustain the notion that Ireland remained an oppressed and unhappy colony of England.[10]

Smith also shared the unionist conviction that the merits or otherwise of any Irish parliament must not rest solely on the assumption of what it might achieve for *Ireland*. The consequences of Irish separation on the rest of the United Kingdom were equally worthy of consideration. Smith mentioned a number of factors deemed worthy of concern, such as the position of English, Scottish, and Anglo-Irish landlords under a Dublin legislature. Believing that the historical record of Ireland's landlords had been the victim of contrived falsehoods, any Irish parliament would quickly become a "robber parliament."[11] Property rights and constitutional safeguards, he concluded, would mean little to "courts, an army and a police controlled by the leaders of the land league."[12]

Every objection to an Irish parliament cited by Smith was reinforced, moreover, by a conviction that what Parnell and the leadership of the Home Rule Federation actually coveted was not 'Home Rule' at all, but an independent Irish republic. Republicanism, after all, had a long and honoured tradition in Irish nationalist circles, and not a few Home Rulers had earned their apprenticeship in the Young Ireland movement and Fenian Brotherhood. Any republic, or anything remotely resembling such an entity, would inevitably pose a considerable, even fatal, challenge to British security. It was, after all, as Smith never tired of pointing out, geo-political realities that had kept England in Ireland these many centuries. Given the unhappy legacy of Anglo-Irish relations, and the craft of nationalist propagandists and agitators, Britain would immediately be faced with the dilemma of a hostile nation sitting immediately off its coast.

If the fates had been kinder, England and Ireland would never have been situated within a thousand miles of each other, and the two islands would have plied their trade and developed their political and religious institutions without the one concerning itself with the other. As facts stood, however, England and Ireland had been "so linked together by destiny that they must be united or enemies." No third possibility existed. "If separation comes now it will be a separation of hatred, with all the consequences to England of a hostile nation at her side; to Ireland, of an enemy, overwhelmingly superior in power, pointing its guns against its coasts."[13] As had been so frequently the case in centuries past, Ireland would turn to England's continental foes only too eager to help redress this imbalance. The rise of

House of Commons Debates

FOURTH SESSION, FIFTH PARLIAMENT.—49 VIC.

SPEECH OF HON. E. BLAKE, M.P.,

ON

HOME RULE FOR IRELAND.

OTTAWA, MAY 4TH, 1886.

Mr. BLAKE. I rise for a moment to intercept that question, in order to bring before the House another, in which the last House showed a deep concern—I mean the Irish question. In 1880, I spoke my views upon this subject, and expressed my belief and hope that we should at no distant day see a measure of Home Rule granted to Ireland. In the year 1882, the question was moved on the other side of this House. At that time we, on this side, heartily co-operated in order to give the greatest possible weight to the proposed action. Then I spoke at length my opinions upon the whole question, which saves me from the necessity of trespassing now upon the time of this House, and since that time, to the best of my humble power, here and elsewhere, I have aided in the advancement of that cause. Since then a new Canadian House of Commons has been elected, which House has not yet spoken upon the question. Since then great events have transpired in the United Kingdom itself. The people, both of Ireland and Great Britain, have received for the first time a very full measure of representation in Parliament. The Irish people, under that measure of representation, have, by an enormous, an overwhelming majority, pronounced in favor of Home Rule, and the great statesman who leads Her Majesty's Government has recognised the vital necessity of grappling at once with the question; and Her Majesty's Government have, as I ventured to suggest on a former occasion, seen the propriety of themselves formulating a plan for the settlement of that question. Now, Sir a controversy has arisen on some of the more important details of that measure. I do not, myself, admire all these details. For example, admitting the great difficulties, I should yet prefer, to the present plan for the exclusion of Ireland from the management of Imperial affairs in which she is interested, her continued representation for those Imperial purposes in an Imperial Parliament—I should prefer the plan, notwithstanding its great difficulty, of her retaining that share of control. But it needs not to discuss this or any other matters of detail, because it has been expressly and authoritatively stated that none of these points are considered in any way vital to the question which is now before England and before the world. The vital principle now at stake is that of self-government for Ireland in local affairs. This was stated by Mr. Gladstone in his reply to the criticisms on the first reading of the Bill, and he has further and authoritatively declared it by his recent manifesto, which was transmitted to us only yesterday. In that manifesto, he thus speaks:

"As for the means we take the establishment in Dublin of a legislative body, empowered to make laws for Irish, as contra-distinguished from Imperial, affairs. It is with this that we are now busied, and not with details and particulars; their time will come."

He adds:

"We are not debating the amount of Irish contributions to the Empire, of the composition of the legislative body, or the maintenance of representative connection with Westminster. On these questions and many more we may and we may not be at odds, but what we are at this moment debating is the large and far larger question which includes, and I think absorbs, them all—the question whether you will or will not have regard to the prayer of Ireland for the management by herself of affairs specifically and exclusively her own. This and no other is the matter which the House of Commons has at once to decide. If on this matter it speaks with a clear and intelligible voice, I feel the strongest assurance that the others, difficult as some of them are, will nevertheless, with the aid of full discussion and with the aid of a wise and conciliatory spirit, be found capable of a rational and tolerable settlement."

Now, Sir, that Bill to which this manifesto refers, stands for a second reading in a few days, and then that vital question is to be decided. A great excitement has arisen; the Empire has been aroused, not merely the Kingdom, but the Empire. The emotion has passed beyond the seas; it has passed beyond the Empire; the English speaking people outside the bounds of the Empire have been aroused, nay more, the free nations all over the world have been moved. Every eye is at this moment bent on Westminister, and every ear is strained to catch the echoes when they come of the great debate, and to learn the issue of the mighty struggle from beyond. Under these circumstances, marks of sympathy and of admiration have been cabled to the First Minister, and he has responded to them in such a sort as proves conclusively that he regards them, as they must be, helpful to him in the enormous task he has undertaken. We know as well as if we had received it already, what the tone of the reply will be to any such communication as we have on a former occasion addressed, or as other large bodies have addressed, upon this subject. The circumstances are, of course, changed; they are changed since the day we addressed Her Majesty; they are changed as to the position of the question; but they are changed in this particular also, to which I call your special attention. At that time we assumed—and I suppose we are not now prepared to recoil; I am not, at any rate, prepared to recoil from the assumption of our right respectfully to approach the Throne with a view to tender our humble advice and hopes upon a subject of such vital importance to the whole Empire, and to Canada as a part of the Empire. But, Sir, at this time, not merely in other particulars are the circum-

Germany, and the relative decline of British naval power, made this possibility an ominous one indeed. Consequently, even if all other unionist objections to Gladstone's initiative could be reasoned away, military security alone made such an initiative as Irish Home Rule unthinkable.

He was also adamant that the threat to Britain did not actually require that an independent Ireland be actively belligerent in any European crisis. It merely required that it sit aside and do nothing. Smith was fully aware of the Admiralty's concern over the possible lack of access to Ireland's strategically-significant ports in time of war. Situated as it was on the western flank of Great Britain, Ireland commanded all the sea routes by which millions of pounds worth of supplies were brought into England. Unable to feed its large urban populations from domestic produce alone, enemy control of these waters would soon bring England to its knees through starvation. If the British Liberal Party and its followers remained oblivious to this, England's continental challengers did not. "There is not one of the enemies of British power and influence in France, Russia...or any part of the world," Smith noted, who did not wish Gladstone godspeed. The introduction of such a bill could only be done by its proponents collectively closing their eyes to the lessons of the past.[14]

That Gladstone and the British Liberal Party *did* choose to close their eyes to the dangers of Home Rule could, in Smith's estimation, only be comprehended in terms of blind political ambition. "Is it possible by any stretch of charity," he argued, "to doubt that Gladstone's failure in 1885 to obtain a majority independent of the Parnellites was the approximate cause of his sudden accession to Home Rule?."[15] Such being the case, Smith argued that, in all of British history, there existed few examples of such an abandonment of principle. To think that Britons had laboured for generations to make their country first among nations, and the envy of Europe, Gladstone's Irish initiative was nothing less than incredible. After all its accomplishments, this was how Britain was to lose its standing among nations. "What a scene it is," he wrote to Tyndall in November of 1885. "What a collapse of old English worth and honour! It is like seeing a famous ship, after all her storms and battles, go down in a dead calm."[16] All for the sake of momentarily capturing the Irish vote!

This same factor, he concluded, accounted for the support expressed for Irish Home Rule in Canada and the United States. Across each country such support as there was depended largely upon the approximate size and influence of the Irish vote in any given electoral district. In those regions where Irish Catholics were of negligible political clout, he argued, support for Home Rule was non-existent. If not for the influence of the Irish ballot in a number of important urban centres, politicians wouldn't have paid the slightest attention to Catholic Ireland's latest point of grievance. "You see the effect of the Irish vote, even on Canadian politics," he wrote to Lord Farrer. "Not one man in ten--probably not one in twenty--of those who voted for the resolutions cared a rush for Home Rule." They were all pandering to the Irish ballot.[17] Moreover, Blake and company had conveniently overlooked the dichotomy between the public face of the pro-Home Rule campaign in Canada and its private face. In Anglo-Protestant Canada it was in the interest of the Fenian and Land Leaguer to show the face of moderation and extend the promise of reconciliation. Only by so doing could they continue to fool so many otherwise responsible politicians. In Montreal, however, "where Roman Catholicism has everything under its feet," the same caution was not deemed necessary. At a meeting of the Young Irishmen's Literary and Benevolent Society in that city, noted Smith, an address by a prominent American Fenian, "brought by special invitation from New York," offered a truer reflection of the movement in Canada.

> He first pours a torrent of rabid invective on Great Britain and her people. Then he justifies, in the frankest terms and with much hilarity, the murder of landlords. His sentiments are greeted with loud applause and laughter, and a vote of thanks to the speaker is moved in the most complimentary

of terms by the Secretary of the Nationalist League.

No honest politician could be deluded by such "palpably feigned moderation," the word for which had been "audibly given by the leader, and which, where the Fenian movement is strong, is not observed." Even if one acknowledged that many Canadian proponents of Irish Home Rule were in fact genuine in their expression of peaceful coexistence, it was, after all, American Fenianism--holding to a "fiendish [and] brutish hatred against the British name and race"--that marshalled the movement. The campaign to secure Home Rule for Ireland was nothing less than a campaign to secure an Irish republic and nothing short of that would ever be accepted. Every penny collected in the United States was donated on that understanding, he argued, and American Fenianism would make certain that "an Irish Parliament is true to the bond."[18]

CANADIAN ORANGEISM

Canada's Home Rule advocates also had to contend with the formidable influence of the Loyal Orange Lodge within English Canada. Transplanted to British North America by Ulster immigrants in the years following the Napoleonic Wars, the Orange Lodge served many social purposes in its new setting, but quickly became renowned for its religious and constitutional positions. Aggressively Protestant, it immediately set itself up as the defender of Canadian Protestantism, and as the self-declared watchdog of the Roman Catholic Church. Aggressively British, it also pledged its considerable membership to champion the British connection and challenge any signs of incipient republicanism. With an ultramontane Quebec to the east, and an anti-British republic to the south, the Order found no shortage of threats. Canada was British, and the Order charged that it would remain so only if its sons and daughters remained vigilant.

The Canadian Order also maintained close ties with its parent body in Ireland. Founded in 1795

13

in the town of Armagh, the Irish Lodge had originally pledged itself to defend the Protestant (Anglican) Ascendancy in Ireland against all challengers, and to maintain the British link. In the ensuing decades, however, several factors determined that the composition and purpose of the Lodge would change. The Act of Union, Catholic Emancipation, and the rise of a Roman Catholic nationalism forcefully reminded Protestants of their common interests and loyalties. Methodists, Baptists, and, most importantly, Presbyterians now sat alongside Anglicans in the local Lodge. Past injustices administered by the Anglican establishment were now forgiven in the wake of a new threat, the revitalisation of a political Catholicism. Feeling themselves besieged by the

AID FOR THE

LOYALISTS OF IRELAND.

In pursuance of the resolutions passed at the great public meeting held in Toronto on March 3th, the Committee of the Loyal and Patriotic Union appeals to all who are true to the Mother Country and the Union, without distinction of party or race, for subscriptions in aid of the Loyal and Unionist cause in Ireland. The treasurers of the fund are: Rev. Dr. John Potts, 33 Elm street, Toronto; Rev. Dr. Joseph Wild, 175 Jarvis street, Toronto; Rev. Prof. Wm. Clark, Trinity College, Toronto; E. F. Clarke, 33 Adelaide street West, Toronto. By any one of these gentlemen or at the Bank of Toronto subscriptions will be received. All subscriptions of whatever amount will be welcomed as proof of goodwill to the cause, and will be severally acknowledged. Friends of the cause throughout the country are invited to organize in their own localities for the purpose of collecting subscriptions.

GOLDWIN SMITH,   JAS. L. HUGHES,
    Chairman.   Secretary.

March 15th, 1886.

Irish majority, Protestants saw the Home Rule initiative as the Catholic Church's latest attempt at usurping their liberties and breaking the British connection. Despite all the moderate talk about national reconciliation, Home Rule would mean 'Rome Rule'. The Roman hierarchy knew it to be such; Protestants should likewise.

In March of 1886, therefore, Canadian Orangemen joined with Smith and other prominent Torontonians in establishing a 'Loyal and Patriotic Union', and in calling together a mass gathering to express the loyalist position on Home Rule. The Loyal and Patriotic Union was established for the sole purpose of countering the pro-Home Rule initiative in Canada. Of particular concern to its organisers was the imminent passage, in the House of Commons, of Blake's resolution expressing Canadian support for Gladstone's bill. If such a representation of Canadian opinion made its way to England unchallenged it could conceivably give Gladstone's bill the final push it needed to succeed. At a mass rally held in Toronto's Temperance Hall in early March, the following counter-resolution was passed for communication to the British press.

> That by expressions of opinion in favour of Home Rule, emanating from an anti-British party in the community, Canadian sentiment has been greatly misrepresented, and that, in our opinion, the Canadian people generally are heartily loyal to the Mother Country, and would regard anything tendering to her dismemberment with the deepest sorrow and shame.

A subsequent resolution stated that "as citizens of the British Empire, we feel a deep interest in its unity and greatness, and enter here our earnest protest against any measure which would dissolve or weaken the Union between Great Britain and Ireland." The third resolution, after expressing admiration for the courage of the Irish minority, swore to "cordially afford them any aid in our power at a crisis fraught with the greatest danger, not only to the integrity of the United

Kingdom, but the British civilisation throughout the world."[19] The resolutions were easily passed. The next day the *Sentinel* claimed that no less than two thousand 'loyalists' had filled the hall, with an additional five thousand being turned away.[20]

In the weeks ahead the Loyal and Patriotic Union circulated an ad in various Toronto newspapers calling on all those opposed to Irish separatism to become active. For those interested in helping finance the opposition of Irish unionists, an account had been opened at the Bank of Toronto.[21] As for the *Orange Sentinel*, and its ideological colleagues, it continued labouring away at Gladstone's initiative until its eventual defeat in the British House of Commons.

TIME AND CIRCUMSTANCE

For his part, Edward Blake had Canada's Irish Catholic population supporting his efforts. Although having arrived in Canada in considerably smaller numbers than in the United States, Canada's Irish Catholics were no less concerned about the welfare of their ancestral home. In the 1880s most would have been either Irish-born or first-generation Canadians and enjoyed hegemony over a number of organisations which they successfully exploited in the cause of Irish Home Rule. The Ancient Order of Hibernians and the Irish-Canadian press were put into service, as was the Roman Catholic Church, which was, outside the province of Quebec, essentially an Irish church. The official Roman Catholic press in English Canada also took up the cause. There was also a degree of support from French Canada, which, despite its resentment of the rising fortunes of Irish Canadians in what had traditionally been 'their' church, saw reflections of their own struggle in Irish Home Rule. (These important themes will be addressed at much greater length in chapters 6 and 7).

The Home Rule cause also had the benefits of time and circumstance on its side. Despite the fact that the overwhelming majority of English Canadians were Protestant, and anti-Catholicism was very much a part of Victorian culture, the Irish cause in Canada was propelled forward by several other factors. Most significantly, there was the increasing influence of the Irish vote in Canadian elections. Alongside those politicians who supported the Irish cause out of principle, there existed those who were indifferent to Home Rule, or mildly supportive of Home Rule, but pragmatic enough to know that supporting Home Rule just might pay off at election time. If the Irish voter was sufficiently pleased by the support offered to Parnell, while the Protestant majority was not sufficiently bothered, there was little to lose.

Those Canadians who did sympathise with the perceived plight of Ulster's Protestants were also handicapped by the Ulstermen's threat of armed resistance should any Home Rule settlement be imposed on the North. Not only was rebellion against lawful authority immensely problematic for many, but it was only one year since a similar rebellion against lawful authority, on the part of the Metis of Manitoba, had been forcefully suppressed--and at the encouragement of none other than the Orange Lodge. The highly controversial execution of the rebellion's leader, Louis Riel, still hung over the Canadian political scene when Ulster's Orangemen were threatening their own uprising. "It will not do," announced the *Canada Presbyterian,* "to shoot down insurgents on the banks of the Saskatchewan and encourage insurrection in Ulster."[22] Regardless of the merits or demerits of Home Rule, if parliament passed Gladstone's bill, it was "the duty of the loyal Christian men of Ulster to bow to the will of the nation."[23] If nothing else, consistency demanded that the Ulstermen not be given privileged treatment.

Opponents of Home Rule were also burdened with the mixed blessing of having Goldwin Smith occupy centre stage in the unionist crusade. If Smith was anything he was controversial, not least because of the adamancy with which he adhered to racial stereotyping. The 19th century was certainly a racist era, but Smith often caused his associates some embarrassment by stating publicly what others stated privately. It was easier, therefore, for advocates of Home Rule to portray unionists in Canada as simple bigots. The fact that Orangemen and Goldwin Smith had formed a pact against Home Rule also smacked of opportunism to some. While the Orange Lodge was the most enthusiastic defender of king and empire in Canada, Goldwin Smith was an advocate of continental union with the United States. Their constitutional positions couldn't have been more diametrical, and it was known that neither one entertained much respect for the other. There was inevitably some public cynicism, therefore, when they joined hands to combat Home Rule, and Home Rulers quickly exploited this perception. Adding to this was the fact that, while Catholic opinion in Canada was united behind Home Rule, Protestant opinion was divided. Blake himself was a Protestant of Irish background. The Toronto *Globe*, and several other uncompromisingly Protestant papers, had also offered their support. As the years passed, however, this advantage would wither away. Although this was not totally apparent in 1892 the seeds of decline were already there, and by 1912 the nationalist cause would actually be on the defensive.

--CHAPTER TWO--

THE SECOND HOME RULE BILL (1892-3)

In the years between the defeat of the first Irish bill and the introduction of the second, the United Kingdom was governed by a Conservative government. Its approach to the Irish unrest was two-fold: the implementation of economic reforms combined to a forceful defence of law and order. While moving quickly to alleviate the worst grievances of the Irish peasantry the government was no longer prepared to tolerate the escalation of agrarian unrest, particularly the murder of isolated landlords and the destruction of livestock. The government made no attempt to conceal the pragmatism at the core of its policy. Convinced that the Irish Question was essentially an economic question, it had resolved to kill Home Rule 'with kindness'. Take away the grievances of the peasantry, and the bitterness so readily exploited by nationalist politicians would soon evaporate. It was for this reason, however, that nationalist politicians often greeted such economic reform packages with ill-disguised suspicion. The government had stated quite clearly what it hoped the end result of its reforms would be, and Irish politicians were not prepared to let that happen. It was partially due to this factor that it was the reverse side of the Conservative coin, namely coercion, which was given the greater emphasis by Irish nationalists, both at home and abroad. In Canada, Irish Canadians successfully introduced anti-coercion resolutions into the federal House of Commons and the provincial legislatures of Ontario and Quebec. These same resolutions made no mention of the reform packages introduced into Ireland, but stated their desire to see Gladstone's Irish bill resurrected as soon as possible.

Although the Conservative government had no intention of succumbing to overseas pressure, Home Rule's prospects changed overnight with the re-election of William Gladstone in 1892. Once returned to office he let it be known that a second Home Rule bill would soon be introduced into the House of Commons. In the United Kingdom and Canada alike the old arguments were raised again in advocacy of, and opposition to, Home Rule. What distinguished the second Home Rule debate from the first, however, were two developments that, in their essence, had little to do with the merits or demerits of Home Rule. The first development was a sex scandal involving Charles Parnell, the undisputed leader of the Home Rule movement, and the organisational disarray that followed his dismissal from the party leadership. The second was the romantic appeal of Edward Blake's decision to accept an Irish seat in the British House of Commons to help resuscitate the Irish cause. These two factors, and not the repetition of the old arguments pro and con, are what distinguished the Irish debate in Canada in 1892-3. While the arguments of 1886 were once again advanced with considerable zeal, these new elements had changed the context within which these arguments had to be presented.

'OUR MODERN KNIGHT'

As mentioned a major factor keeping Canadian eyes focused on the Irish Question after 1892 was Edward Blake's election to the British House of Commons as a nationalist member for the Irish riding of South Longford. Discouraged by the defeat of the Canadian Liberal Party in two consecutive elections, Blake had resigned the leadership and gone off to Europe to restore his failing health. Further removing Blake from Canadian politics was the fact that, under the party's new leader, Wilfrid Laurier, the Liberals had adopted a policy of unrestricted reciprocity with the United States, a policy which Blake strongly disapproved of. When the offer came from the anti-Parnellite section of the Irish Party of an Irish seat in the British House of Commons, therefore, he quickly accepted. While Blake's Canadian admirers, and those who agreed with him on the Irish issue, wished him well in his Irish career, they understood that his absence could possibly hurt the Home Rule cause in Canada. Others, however, believed that, far from hurting the pro-Home Rule lobby in Canada, the idea of a Canadian statesman returning to the land of his forebearers to champion its struggle for liberty had considerable romantic appeal.

For many Canadians, moreover, the romanticism of Blake's crusade served as a welcome antidote to the demoralisation of the Home Rule cause in Canada in the wake of the Parnell scandal. In 1890 Charles Parnell, 'Ireland's uncrowned king', had been named in a divorce suit by one Captain O'Shea as being his wife's lover. When the full story emerged it was revealed that the situation was even more disastrous than thought. Parnell, it appeared, had not only had a long-term affair with Mrs O'Shea, but had actually fathered her children. Not surprisingly, the effect on Catholic opinion in Ireland, and, equally important, Nonconformist opinion in England, was devastating. While the Catholic hierarchy denounced Parnell from the pulpit, Gladstone announced that he could not continue to support the Irish Party with an admitted adulterer at its helm. The Irish Party divided over what to do with the issue, but it was a clear majority of Irish MPs who voted to remove Parnell from the leadership.[24] As for Parnell, he had adamantly refused to acknowledge the majority vote and step down. The party might depose him but he and his supporters would carry the fight into the next election. When the election was finally called pro-Parnell and anti-Parnell candidates faced each other across the country. The result was bitter division and the demoralisation of the entire movement. Within months of the election Parnell was dead. His health had never been good, and the strain and exertion of recent years had taken their toll.[25]

The Parnell sex scandal and its accompanying divisions served, moreover, to turn many away from Irish politics altogether. In its place Irish nationalists sought fulfilment in the study of the ancient origins of Irish society. A Gaelic League was founded in 1893 that dissociated itself entirely from politics, preferring instead to lead a struggle against the Anglicisation of Irish *culture*. Not only was the Irish language to be studied, but Irish music, dress, poetry, and art forms were to be restored to their rightful place in Irish life. Meanwhile the Gaelic Athletic Association was undertaking the same objective in sports, while others, such as W.B. Yeats, sought to direct Irish energies into a literary renaissance. While this boded well for Irish culture, it was a conscious and popular, if temporary, repudiation of political nationalism.

Moreover, while the Irish Party was in a state of disarray, Ulster's Protestants were better organised than ever before, and mass demonstrations took place across the province in opposition to Home Rule. (At the unionist convention in Belfast in 1892 nearly 2000 delegates carried a resolution which promised to resist Home Rule with physical force.) In the House of Commons, where nationalist support was divided and demoralised, Ulster's supporters in the Conservative Party were as forceful as ever. Furthermore, the intervening years between the first and second Home Rule bills had seen Ireland governed by a Tory administration determined to undermine agitation for Home Rule by addressing the most urgent of Irish grievances. By the time 1892 arrived many of the reform measures that the Irish Party had insisted must wait for Home Rule had already been successfully implemented--and *by a unionist government*. One result, therefore, was to weaken the nationalists' claim that London was incapable of providing sound government in Ireland. These factors all served to dishearten the nationalist movement in Ireland, as did the knowledge that, should the second bill succeed in passing the House of Commons, it would surely be vetoed by the Lords.

These factors also served to demoralise Irish sympathisers in Canada. Even the most enthusiastic advocates of the Irish cause were united in their condemnation of Parnell, and in their assertion that he must step down. "Mr. Parnell," reported the *Toronto Globe*, "has been overcome by a Delilah, who happens to be another man's wife." Even if he chose to marry Mrs. O'Shea, "the scandal in which he has entangled himself must result, if not in his withdrawal from public life, at any rate in his retirement from the Irish leadership." It was inevitable, it insisted, "that Mr. Gladstone will insist on a change."[26] When Gladstone did demand Parnell's resignation, and Parnell flatly refused to even consider such a move, Canadian opinion was shocked. Was the Irish leader insufficiently aware of the weightiness of his transgression? Was he really willing to put his own vanity ahead of the welfare of the Irish cause? Was this the man whom millions of Irish adored as their gallant, selfless leader, their uncrowned king? "Mr. Parnell," concluded the *Victoria Daily Colonist*, "is not proving himself the pure and disinterested patriot that his admirers believed him to be. He, and every one else who is able to think, must see that a disagreement between Mr. Gladstone and him must be injurious, if not fatal, to the cause of Home Rule."[27] When Parnell was deposed by his own party members, but insisted on remaining actively involved in politics, it only served to further disillusion Home Rule's friends in Canada. Parnell, added the *Colonist*, "by his own evil deeds, has forfeited his claim to the respect of good men everywhere."[28]

It was this sense of demoralisation that many Canadians hoped Blake's Irish adventure might rectify. The public interest in Blake's Irish career was heightened further by suggestion that he might be offered a post of some importance. Under the heading, "Our Modern Knight," the *Vancouver Daily World* predicted the following in June of 1892.

> It will not be inappropriate did Mr. Blake heal the strife between the jarring factions and raise himself to a position of the greatest prominence in the councils of the party. Another point of view which will interest Canadians is the possibility, nay probability, of Mr. Blake becoming a Minister of the Crown.[29]

The appeal of Blake's crusade again appeared formidable when he paid a return visit to Canada in September of 1892. A rally organised for him in Toronto's Horticultural Pavilion had 4000 in attendance, with several hundred others being turned away. Speaking before the great crowd he again asserted his belief that "four-fifths and more of our people, from Halifax to Vancouver, favoured Home Rule for Ireland." If Canadians avoided confusing the issue at hand by "the introduction of any such questions as those of

race, of creed, or of local politics, Canada as a
whole could on this subject speak with an all but
absolutely unanimous voice." Such a voice, he
asserted, would be "potent towards the success of
the struggle." It was imperative, therefore, that

NO HOME RULE.

A Monster Gathering in the Auditorium.

MR. BLAKE IS ANSWERED.

Eloquent Addresses by Visiting Irishmen.

THE UNIONIST SIDE OF THE QUESTION

creed and partisanship be kept out of the matter
altogether, and to unite "all the elements which
might make that voice as strong, as clear, as
harmonious as possible." He recognised that there
existed in Canada "a few opponents of Home Rule,"

but insisted that their fears were unfounded. "It is emphatically not a measure of separation, or disintegration or decay, but a measure healing and restorative, creating for the first time a union worthy of the name."[30]

Reporting on the demonstration, the *Toronto Globe*, a consistent advocate of Irish Home Rule, described the rally as a "brilliant success," and as "exceedingly gratifying to the friends of the system of self-government which Canadians enjoy, and to all those who desired to see honour done to an eminent Canadian who has given a quarter of a century of unremitting toil to the service of his native land." What particularly impressed the editors of the *Globe*, was the cross-denominational and bipartisan consensus that had apparently coalesced around the Home Rule issue in Canada. "Noone," it insisted, "could have failed to remark on the thoroughly representative character of the gathering." On the platform were seen "Protestant ministers and bishops and priests of the Roman Catholic Church; Liberals and Conservatives; the advisers of the Crown both in Provincial and Federal affairs; members of the Legislature and of both branches of the Dominion Parliament--men whose loyalty is impeachable, and who have, by their scrupulous regard for the rights of the minority in Canada, given guarantees for the sincerity of their avowal of scrupulous regard for the rights of the minority in Ireland."[31]

The *Ottawa Citizen* was equally impressed with the meeting, but for different reasons. For one, it was a sign of Canada's maturity and the respect in which its citizens were held throughout the empire. "It is but just that Canada should make a return for the attentive oversight which British Statesmen have exercised over our progress," it announced, "and no return could be more appropriate than the contribution of a public man of superior capacity and colonial experience."[32] Canada was finally in the position of benefactor, bringing new insight and new energies to bear on the empire's oldest dilemma, that of Ireland. But the *Citizen* insisted that, to be fully effective, Blake had to serve a second purpose. By holding fast to the Canadian analogy of dual representation--provincial and federal--Blake must steer Gladstone away from the one fatal flaw in his Irish legislation: the reduction or elimination of Irish representation at Westminster. Blake, it insisted, could do "a great service to Mr. Gladstone and the empire...by pointing out in the British parliament the vital necessity in case of Home Rule of a strong Irish representation at Westminster." Gladstone, part of whose original scheme "was the abolition altogether of Irish representation in the Imperial parliament, and who is now reported to be determined at least to reduce it, could not make a more fatal mistake for Great Britain."

> If Ireland has no voice in Imperial interests and control, Ireland will care nothing for the empire. Home Rule will develop into the be-all and end-all of Ireland, resulting in a new and eventually irresistible agitation for entire separation from Britain. If Britain wants to hold Ireland in firm alliance, Britain must insist on Ireland taking a full share of the responsibilities and reaping a full share of the honours of the empire.[33]

In this regard would Blake offer a great service to Britain and the empire.

But not everyone was impressed by the Blake rally, or, for that matter, any aspect of his involvement in Irish politics. His critics even included many Canadians who supported Home Rule in principle. Such persons, while wishing Gladstone godspeed in his campaign, were critical of Blake for deeming it his business to interfere in British affairs, for having deemed Irish politics a legitimate topic for discussion in Canadian legislatures, and for serving to retard the healing of racial and religious divisions within Canada itself. No journal was more critical of Blake in this matter than the *Toronto World*. "Why," it asked, "should bitterness and rancour be engendered between two sections of the community here about the condition of affairs in a country three thousand miles away? Was there such an absence of statesmanship, such entire ignorance of the science of government in Great Britain "that Canada needs step in and teach men who have the wisdom of ages to fall back upon how to do it? The *World* thinks not, and has always thought so." Particularly annoying was Blake's decision to accept the invitation to speak on the Irish matter upon his return to Canada. If the *Globe* admired Blake for his appeal for bi-partisan and cross-denominational support for Home Rule, others accused Blake of reckless naiveté. "If a reawakening of faction and a revival of religious discord should follow the demonstration in honour of Mr. Blake," argued the *World* "the responsibility will rest upon that gentleman." It was bad enough for him to go to Britain and advance the Irish cause there, but to bring Irish disputes back to Canada was another. An intelligent man, Blake surely knew that old animosities in Canada would certainly be rekindled by the Irish debate. "Already Mr. Blake's needless action has begot opposition from the other side and it threatens to rage hotly for the remainder of the season...until some other agitator comes along to give it new life."[34]

These criticisms, harsh as they were, came from those persons who were either supportive of, or simply indifferent to, Irish Home Rule. As the *World* noted, however, word of the upcoming Blake rally had also mobilised those Canadians who were wholly opposed to Home Rule. The largest unionist rally of the period took place in Toronto the night following the Blake demonstration. In attendance were many prominent Canadians, as well as prominent Ulstermen over for a pan-Presbyterian conference being held in Toronto. The clergymen took the opportunity to challenge Blake's contention that only the privileged classes, remnants of the old Protestant Ascendancy in Ireland, were opposed to Home Rule. They reminded the audience, and members of the press, that the most enthusiastic opponents of Gladstone's measure were not Anglican Churchmen, who might be suspected of Ascendancy biases, but Irish Presbyterians. Resented by the Anglican establishment, Irish Presbyterians, like their Roman Catholic neighbours, had struggled under the injustices of the penal laws so frequently cited by Blake. It was for this reason, they asserted, that Irish Presbyterians were resolved not to permit *another* ascendancy, this time a Roman Catholic one, from establishing itself in Ireland.

The speakers at the rally also took Blake to task for his continued references to the Canadian Analogy, and his alleged indifference to the hard facts of the matter. One of the many resolutions passed at the rally went as follows.

> That this meeting disavows and repudiates the claims publicly expressed by the Hon. Edward Blake and others of the Liberal Party in England that there is any real analogy between the system of constitutional government in Canada and the proposed system of Home Rule for Ireland, and that this meeting further expresses the well-founded misapprehension that Home Rule in Ireland as now understood would tend to the disruption of the British Empire and destroy that unity and prestige which command influence in all parts of the world.[35]

For their part, Home Rule's Canadian supporters were dismissive of the unionist critique. Referring to the prominent personalities in attendance, the Toronto *Globe* insisted that not even this advantage could give "freshness or originality to mere rehearsals of assertions with which every Canadian who reads the newspapers and reviews is thoroughly familiar." Nor could they "invest with authority opinions put forth without sufficient argument, such as that home rulers will be satisfied with nothing less than Rome rule and the separation of Ireland from England."[36] Other Home Rule advocates were even more strident in their criticism.

And yet, despite their confidence, time was moving against the Home Rule cause in English Canada. Already in 1886 the Home Rule lobby, while outwardly formidable, had been forced to settle for a parliamentary resolution of support which was considerably weaker than that of 1882. And although there was another attempt at passing a resolution in 1892, it was a complete failure. And in the United Kingdom itself, the 1892 Home Rule bill, while managing to pass the House of Commons, was speedily vetoed by the House of Lords. A new bill would not be introduced until 1912, by which time Irish Canadians were two decades further along the road to cultural assimilation, and two decades further removed from their ancestral home. Many of the first generation of zealots were dead, dying, or removed from political life. By 1912, moreover, there was a general consensus within English Canada that the Catholic Church was showing a renewed zeal in extending its secular arm, and that Britain's continental challengers were stronger and more confident than ever before. By 1912, therefore, although noone could have foreseen it in 1892, unionist sympathisers were setting the agenda in Canada. Most importantly, the unionist position was being readily embraced in the province of Ontario, the most populous and electorally-significant corner of the dominion.

--CHAPTER THREE--

THE THIRD HOME RULE BILL (1912-18)

On 25 March 1903 George Wyndham, secretary for Ireland in the British government, presented to parliament an Irish reform package unprecedented in its scope. Based on the recommendations of a Land Conference, which had been established to inquire into the matter, the package provided the Canadian equivalent of $60,000,000 toward helping the Irish peasantry purchase Irish estates which, since the days of Cromwell and beyond, had belonged to Anglo-Protestant landlords. A further $100,000,000 was provided in low-interest loans (a number that would soon grow to $150,000,000). According to the *Canadian Annual Review*, the package was "large, statesmanlike and satisfactory to all who were willing to be satisfied."[37] The *Winnipeg Free Press* added the following.

> The Land Purchase Bill gives every promise of solving the Irish question, which has so long demanded settlement...The proposed arrangement takes the form of peasant proprietorship: the land for the people. Part of the money required to bring about this great change is being furnished by the British taxpayer; in addition the credit of Great Britain is pledged to the carrying through of the scheme. With the land question disposed of, the political disquiet in Ireland will disappear in its wake; for agrarian troubles have been the root of Ireland's political troubles.[38]

For the opponents of Irish Home Rule it was hoped that this latest initiative in a long list of reforms granted to Ireland would spell the end of all Home Rule agitation. No Irishman could now argue that Britons were inherently incapable of providing sound government in Ireland. Far from *discouraging* nationalists, however, the Wyndham Act encouraged them to work harder to ensure that the dream of Home Rule would not fade in the wake of the latest reform package. Lest the Conservatives succeed in killing Home Rule 'with kindness' the national question was taken up with a new enthusiasm by its proponents. In the Canadian House of Commons, Irish Canadians, having recovered from the demoralisation of the 1890s, initiated a new Home Rule resolution which handily passed the House on 31 March 1903. Home Rule, its Canadian proponents argued, would cap a generation of magnificent reforms introduced into Ireland. It would be an act of great courage and foresight, securing for the British prime minister the gratitude of history, and of generations of Irish men and women yet to be born. Irish history, they argued, was at a crossroads, and the government should immediately seize the opportunity to do the right thing.

A new Home Rule bill would have to wait eight more years, however, as the Conservative government of the day was firmly opposed to granting Home Rule to Ireland. The Irish Question, it insisted, was an economic question, well on its way to being solved. Continued agitation for a devolved legislature was the work of a small number of vested interests in Ireland, and irreconcilable elements in the United States. Nor was Home Rule revived as an issue, as many hoped it might be, after the Liberal Party's crushing electoral victory of 1906. Such was the extent of the Liberal majority over the next four years that the Irish caucus was completely ineffective in advancing Home Rule. The Irish cause, after all, had done the Liberal Party few favours in the past, and most Liberals were quite content to let the matter lie. Besides, while Ireland had no immediate grievances to speak of, the new government had an ambitious package of reforms that it desired to see passed for the benefit of all citizens of the United Kingdom, not just the residents of Ireland. Simply put, Ireland was not a going concern in British politics between 1906 and 1910.

This reality changed overnight, however, when, in the general election of December 1910, the Irish Nationalist Party once again held the balance of power at Westminster. In return for Irish support in pushing through an ambitious package of tax reform, Herbert Asquith, the new Liberal premier, agreed to the introduction of a third Irish bill. And it appeared that this bill, unlike those of 1886 and 1892, would successfully sail through the British parliament. One of Asquith's reform initiatives, after all, had been the abolition of the Lords' veto power, and its replacement by a limited two-year suspensive veto. A healthy majority in the House of Commons, and a paralysed House of Lords, strongly suggested that Ireland would have its parliament after all--and within two years! Irish nationalists and their sympathisers around the globe were ecstatic.

Unionists, however, were outraged. Never had there been such an abandonment of political principle in the pursuit of power. It was one thing to play politics over the allocation of funds for a new bridge, another to play politics with the British constitution. Insisting that, on such occasions, there were things stronger than parliamentary majorities, Ulster unionists, backed by their Scottish and English supporters, threatened to set up a provisional government to govern Ulster the moment Home Rule was enacted. September 28, 1912 was proclaimed 'Ulster Day' and rallies were held province-wide to express loyalist displeasure. September 28 also witnessed the signing of a 'Solemn League and Covenant' by 450,000 persons committing them to do all in their power to defeat Home Rule. An Ulster Volunteer Force, numbering 100,000 men, was founded to discourage any efforts at coercing unionists out of the existing political arrangement. At first of little military concern, it became a formidable force when 24,000 German rifles and 3,000,000 rounds of ammunition were smuggled into Ulster and successfully dispersed across the province. The strength of the unionists' position was further enhanced when the British government ordered a regiment stationed near Dublin to prepare itself to march north to disarm the Ulstermen. No fewer than fifty-eight officers, the commanding general included, informed London that they would sooner resign than follow that particular order.

If Catholic Ireland was to receive Home Rule it was increasingly apparent to most observers that it was not going to include Ulster, or at least not the predominantly Protestant areas of Ulster. It should be stated, however, that partition was not the objective of unionist resistance at this time, being embraced only as a last resort. Edward Carson, the unquestioned leader of the Ulstermen, was a southern Irishman, MP for Dublin University, and an Irish patriot--if one who believed that Ireland's rightful place was within the United Kingdom. It had been his resolve to keep all of Ireland for the Union, not just Ulster. His main interest in the North was to use the threat of Ulster separatism as his ace card against the Home Rule movement. If Irish nationalists went for Home Rule it would be Home Rule without Ulster. And, in 1912-14, it was a credible card to play. East Ulster was an industrial success story of some magnitude. At the time of the third Irish Bill's introduction, Belfast could boast some of the largest linen-works, rope-works, tobacco plants, and shipyards in the world. Nothing better signified the economic importance of Ulster than the launching of the Titanic from Belfast's Harland and Wolff yards in 1912. As unionists saw it, a separate Ireland without Ulster would be economically non-viable. It was Carson's hope that, in light of Ulster's resolve not to belong to any Home Rule state, nationalists would reconsider the merits of unionism. Only if southern Ireland persisted in its separatist agenda would unionists proceed to set up their own state of Northern Ireland.

Unionists justified their actions in the conviction that since Home Rule was the result of partisan manoeuvring in the House of Commons it lacked moral authority. Such a constitutional initiative as Home Rule for Ireland required a greater mandate than that claimed by Asquith. Unionists insisted that they would not permit their political, economic, and religious interests to be sacrificed to ensure Mr. Asquith's short-term career goals. Only if Asquith received the support of the British electorate, by means of a referendum on the issue, would unionists put down their arms and accept Home Rule. If the government refused, and insisted on coercing Ulster, then conflict was inevitable.

Watching the momentum turn against them, nationalists took a page from the Ulstermen and formed their own paramilitary body, the Irish Volunteers, and immediately began importing guns and ammunition from Germany. Ireland was one and indivisible. The Irish nation had voted for Home Rule and the cause needed no other mandate. Neither the British electorate nor an armed minority in the north of Ireland had the right to obstruct the march of Irish democracy. Civil war appeared to be a distinct possibility in the British Isles for the first time since the 17th century. When an emergency meeting called by the king at Buckingham Palace failed to find common ground, many prepared for the worst. The situation was saved only by the commencement of hostilities on the continent in August of 1914. The Home Rule debate was shelved for the war's duration and Irishmen--Catholic and Protestant alike--marched off to kill and die for Britain. The Catholics marched off to Belgium in the hope of winning English gratitude, and to show that an autonomous Ireland would remain a friendly Ireland. Protestants marched off to prove their eternal loyalty to king and country.

ENGLISH CANADIANS AND CATHOLICISM

The dynamics of the Home Rule debate within English Canada roughly paralleled that of the United Kingdom, with the pro-unionist lobby clearly setting the agenda. It is not that there was a marked decline in support for Home Rule in Canada--there remained significant editorial support in the Canadian press--but it was certainly less vitalic. The zeal of the first generation of Home Rulers in Canada had burned out. Edward Blake was dead, and most of his earlier colleagues in the cause were either dead, dying, or retired from politics. The Liberal Party which had governed Canada from 1895 to 1911 had been tossed out of office on a cry of 'treason' for its efforts to negotiate a free trade agreement with the United States. Such a deal, its critics charged, was a step towards the annexation of Canada by the United States. The Conservative Party that had replaced it had come to power on a platform of ultra-loyalism and fealty to empire. Nobody was going to go about raising a resolution in support of Irish Home Rule under this administration. To the contrary, every reference to the Irish Question in the House of Commons during these years pertained to support for Edward Carson and the Ulster Volunteers.

Contributing to this metamorphosis was the spectre of Roman Catholic triumphalism engendered by two recently promulgated, and highly publicised, papal decrees. The first, *Motu Propriu*, was pronounced in 1908 and was aimed at forbidding any Catholic from taking their priest, or any priest of the church, before a civil court on any matter without the consent of their bishop. Regardless of the severity of the crime committed by the priest, it was to be kept out of the secular courts. To Protestants, and liberal-minded Catholics, this was unacceptable interference in the legal system of every democratic state. Anti-papal sentiment flared further with the release of yet another Vatican promulgation shortly thereafter. The second decree, *Ne Temere*, was pronounced three years later on the matter of mixed marriages. It reiterated the Vatican's position that such marriages were not recognised by the church, and that those living in such an arrangement lived in a state of adultery. The marriage was invalid, and the Roman Catholic partner could leave that marriage without committing a sin. The universal response of Protestant opinion was that such doctrines were unconscionable. The decree was not only a crime against the institution of marriage, however, but an affront to the entire legal structure of the Canadian state. Who would determine on what grounds a marriage was valid in Canada, the Canadian government or the pope?

After 1908, therefore, Protestant opinion in Canada was aroused in opposition to what was envisioned as a reinvigorated political Catholicism. For many it was further evidence that the Catholic Church had not come to terms with its loss of political power since the Reformation, and that it was determined to reassert its secular arm wherever it could. Many feared that even the Liberal Party of Canada had fallen under the influence of the Catholic hierarchy. Evidence of this, it was asserted, could be found in the unprecedented step of permitting the Catholic Church to hold its Eucharistic Congress in Montreal in 1910. It was also significant to many that Wilfrid Laurier had given his Catholic ministers permission to participate in the Eucharistic procession in their official robes. Most telling, however, was Laurier's refusal to rebuke Chief Justice Gironard for offering "the homage of Canada" to the papal legate. When the federal Liberal party was ejected from office in 1911 the *Orange Sentinel*, with perhaps some justification, stated that the results could be put down to "an aroused Protestantism."[39]

It was, in part, because of these domestic concerns that many Canadian Protestants now followed Irish developments with heightened interest. No longer did the old Orange cry that Home Rule meant 'Rome Rule' seem so paranoid. At the same time British assurances that the religious liberties of the Protestant minority would be guaranteed by London no longer seemed so reliable. Ottawa had been granted powers of disallowance under the British North America Act, reminded one prominent Orangeman in 1912, but its use of the Veto had been substantially abandoned in yet another attempt to placate Roman Catholic Quebec.[40] And once a legislature was granted to Dublin, no British government would be willing to implement its disallowance options. London's anxiety to woo American public opinion at this time of international unrest made this a virtual certainty. Home Rule would definitely mean Roman domination of Ireland's Protestants, and that was unconscionable. Speaking before a large gathering of Orangemen in Toronto, Thomas Crawford, former Speaker of the Ontario legislature, stated that "the situation in Ireland becomes a matter of very great importance not only to Orangemen but to Protestants. It is not a question of political party. It is a question of the submersion of [Ireland]...to be ruled and influenced by a central authority in the papal chair."[41] Home Rule, insisted another, was not about the enlargement of the liberties of the Irish people under a free parliament, but "the creation of a papal State...where British law and justice would be superseded by the Canon Law of the Papacy as is the case in the Province of Quebec in this Dominion."[42]

ENGLISH CANADIANS AND EMPIRE

In putting its case across to the Canadian public the pro-unionist movement also had the added benefit of worrisome developments in international relations. Whereas in 1886 and 1892 Great Britain had been the undisputed military and naval power on earth, the ensuing years had witnessed this position deteriorate. If the argument that Home Rule could potentially jeopardise British security interests was dismissed by many during the earlier debates, that privilege had also evaporated. The British government itself had acknowledged its vulnerability by actively searching out foreign alliances for the first time since the early 19th century. Many Canadians, moreover, had also been expressing considerable anxiety over the empire's state of military unpreparedness. The German naval threat, many argued, dictated that the United Kingdom must remain militarily indivisible. Who could say what position an Irish parliament might take in the empire's moment of need. In time of war, what safeguard was there to prevent Dublin from taking advantage of England's difficulties to proclaim an independent republic? This risk was too great for any nation in Britain's situation to take. Ireland, concluded one prominent Toronto politician in 1912, was a "hostile nation which will take advantage of any trouble Britain may be in to attack her." In the empire's time of distress, insisted another, Ireland would surely become "a centre of conspiracy against the integrity of the British Empire, and might lead to the overthrow of British power and influence."[43]

When hostilities commenced on the continent in August of 1914--a mere month before the Asquith bill was to become law--the Orange Lodge seized the occasion to forcefully restate its case to the Canadian public. How could any loyal Canadian, however well intentioned, any longer deny the unionists' military case against Home Rule? Germany's invasion of Belgium, a country ostensibly within Britain's sphere, only emphasised how aggressive England's challengers had become, and how vigilant the empire must remain. With such international predators on the loose it was no time to be discussing independence for Ireland, a country which, in centuries past, had habitually aligned itself with Britain's enemies. And it had to be remembered that Ireland was strategically situated along vital trade routes essential to Britain's very survival in time of war. If ever a neutral or hostile Ireland succumbed to Belgium's fate, England would be lost.

The Order also took advantage of developments in Ireland itself after the declaration of war to emphasise the untrustworthiness of significant numbers within Ireland's majority Catholic population. It also seized the occasion to contrast this unworthiness with the sacrifices made by Ireland's Protestants. At the outbreak of the war Edward Carson had offered the services of the Ulster volunteers, created, at least ostensibly, to do battle against the British Army, to the Asquith government. Twenty-nine thousand members of the Volunteers had entered the British Army as the 36th (Ulster) Division. No greater example of imperial fervour could be found, argued the *Sentinel*, than Ulster's offer of its young men to a government which, in weeks and months passed, had threatened to march its armies through the streets of Belfast. Referring to the sacrifices of the Ulster Division at the Somme in July 1916, the *Sentinel* offered the following tribute to its Irish brethren.

> Magnificent as has been the response of
> Ontario in men, money and support, it
> has been exalted by Ulster. No part of

the Empire has shown greater enthusiasm or made greater sacrifices. And in the field what glory the Ulster Division has won! On the first of July did they not lead the sweep on the German trenches? Their Colonel fell at the outset and hundreds with him. Instead of being appalled at the carnage, it stimulated their determination to conquer, and once again the cry was heard of No Surrender in a death struggle to win victory for the British flag.[44]

In stark contrast, however, was the question mark placed over the loyalties of Ireland's Catholics, particularly in the wake of the republican uprising in Dublin on Easter Monday 1916. While Ulstermen, Britons, and English Canadians were struggling against Prussian militarism in the trenches of France, French Canadians remained hostile to the entire effort, and Ireland's Catholics were again rising against the crown. Not only did this underline the military argument against Irish separatism, but emphasised the injustice in placing Irish Protestants in the care of men who would betray the empire in its moment of need. It was men such

HOME RULE MEASURE MENACE TO EMPIRE

On Eve of Ulster Day Toronto Mass Meetings Oppose Proposed Legislation Granting Ireland Self-Government — Applaud Right Hon. Walter Long's Address.

as these who would seize power in Ireland after Home Rule was enacted. It was the hard republican element who would be the king-makers in any Irish parliament. And if they were not, they would turn once again to the bomb and bullet. "The movement brings out the fact," insisted the *Sentinel*, "that John Redmond's guarantees...are the flimsiest possible grounds upon which the fortunes and fate of Ulster can be entrusted to a Dublin Parliament." In light of the rebellion, "the position of the loyal men of Ulster under Home Rule" could not be gainsaid. It was a clear and unequivocal warning to the government "against the inclusion of Ulster within the sphere of authority of a Dublin Parliament."[45] Military security demanded that all of Ireland be kept for the Union. If, however, the British government could not bring itself to stand up to Irish nationalists, the only alternative was Home Rule without Ulster.

ENGLISH CANADIANS AND...*ENGLAND*

During the period under examination the Orange Lodge was also remarkably successful in exploiting popular resentments within English Canada in turning the tide against Irish nationalism. Simply put, alongside a regenerated imperial sentiment in Canada, there also existed a new sense of grievance against England, or, more correctly, English politicians. This sentiment had never been entirely absent in English Canada, but it had rarely been as strongly felt as in the late Victorian and Edwardian era. They remembered that British politicians had sacrificed Canadian interests in the Webster-Ashburton and Oregon boundary settlements in the pre-confederation era. In 1871 the British had made substantial concessions to the Americans in the fisheries and the navigation of the St. Lawrence, but that same treaty had said nothing about compensation to Canadians for damages inflicted by the Fenian Raids. It was the Alaska boundary dispute of 1903, however, that had the most traumatic impact on Canadian imperialists. No sooner had Canadian sons returned from performing their duty to empire in southern Africa when English politicians were once again compromising Canada's interests. British careerists, it appeared, were all too eager to sacrifice the interests of Canada and empire for short-term benefits, be they economic, diplomatic, or partisan.

Some years ago Carl Berger noted that "one of the most arresting features of Canadian imperialist thought was how seldom praise was lavished upon England."[46] This does not suggest, however, that Canadians did not respect the British people, cherish Canada's British heritage and institutions, and appreciate the protection given the Canadian coast by the Royal Navy. The uproar that issued from many quarters over the Liberals' handling of the naval bill should remind us that many did indeed feel grateful. There was also an acknowledgement that England was the fount of empire and home of the monarchy, and that the empire was essential to the maintenance of Canada's distinctiveness in North America. At the same time, however, these sentiments were offset by the conviction that the protection given Canada was reciprocated by the voluntary undertakings of Canadians in southern Africa, and by the opportunities offered Britons in the Canadian west.

The rising opposition to Irish Home Rule in Canada has to be understood within this political and cultural context. The response of many was also conditioned by the battle just won against that other, *less noble*, brand of imperialism-- American. In congratulating the Conservative leader Robert Borden on his 1911 election victory, and the scuttling of the Canada-US free trade agreement, Ontario's premier, James Whitney, wrote that "No such good work was ever done in British North America before, and having regard to its effects on the future of the Empire I doubt if any one day's work in England in modern times ever signified as much."[47] But as soon as Canadians, particularly Ontarians, had preserved the integrity of empire, Great Britain was again jeopardising it.

The ability of the Loyal Orange Lodge to win the public relations battle within English Canada between 1912-16 is directly related to these developments. The tone, and appeal, of Orange demonstrations across the country makes this apparent. Throughout this period the cause of Ulster was a recurrent theme in Orange parades and protests; by the summer of 1914 it was the sole theme, and the numbers that flocked to the 'Twelfth' demonstrations were unprecedented. Nowhere was this more evident than in Toronto. "Saturday's demonstration in commemoration of the victory of William, Prince of Orange, over James at the Boyne, in Ireland," reported the *Sentinel*, "was the most satisfactory in the history of Canadian Orangeism."[48] The same gathering was described by the *Evening Telegram* as "the greatest parade ever," claiming that as many as two hundred thousand had lined the parade's route "like an army assembling for the morrow's battle."[49] The *Toronto Daily Star* recorded the day's events under the heading, "PARADE BIGGEST AND MOST SERIOUS EVER,"[50] while the *Toronto World* noted that the twelve thousand Orangemen who walked to Exhibition Park "were the largest gathering of Orangemen that the Glorious Twelfth has ever brought together in Toronto."[51]

The seriousness that the *Star* referred to derived from the fact that Canadian Orangemen, as well as considerable numbers of others, saw in the actions of the Asquith government the English traits of which they had long despaired. It was unconscionable that Ulstermen should be rewarded for their sacrifices for king and empire by being sacrificed to the cross of convenience. The anger felt by many over London's latest act of infidelity was real, and not a few expressed support for the Ulstermen's resolve to take up arms, should the need arise, to convince the Liberal government of the folly of its ways. In July of 1914 the *Toronto Globe* reported on one of the many pro-Carson rallies as follows.

> "Hands off Ulster" was the burden of all the speeches at Markdale at the big Grey County Orange celebration yesterday, which was attended by 1,500 Orangemen of fifty lodges, and which

> drew the largest number of people that
> has ever been in that town. The temper
> of all the Orangemen with respect to
> the Irish problem and the fate of
> Ulster...was manifest in the enthusiasm
> that was evinced as speaker after
> speaker addressed the mass gathering
> and exhorted them to lend their moral
> support to those who opposed Home Rule.
> The references, lightly veiled, to the
> possibility of the harsh arbitrament of
> arms also met with ringing applause.[52]

Orangemen were, moreover, preparing (or at least threatening) to send a contingent of one thousand volunteers to Belfast should hostilities erupt. Whether or not there was much substance to this, it was of sufficient concern to some that it was raised in the House of Commons by a concerned member of the opposition.[53] Another protested the presence of another member of the governing party at a pro-Carson rally in Toronto.[54] More serious was the revelation that the member for York Centre, an officer in the Canadian militia, had sent a telegram of support to Sir Edward Carson in Belfast. It read, in part, as follows.

> Thousands of loyal Canadians are with
> you in your magnificent fight to
> preserve the best traditions of British
> citizenship by resisting the coercion
> of Ulster. We are ready, if necessary,
> to help you with men and money to the
> last ditch.[55]

There may not have been much substance to such bravado, but prominent Canadian Orangemen, including the Reverend H.A. Fish, grand chaplain of British North America, and Fred Dane, Canadian trade commissioner to Glasgow, were in northern Ireland assuring assembled Orangemen that financial and material support, as well as men, were indeed available. "Brother Fred Dane," noted the *Daily Mail and Empire*, "said that the same Orange lodges...that furnished men for the war in

South Africa were able and willing to give troops to Ulster when needed."[56]

If anyone was to blame for the present crisis, continued the *Mail and Empire*, it was premier Asquith. He had been fully cognisant of the bitter divisions that the introduction of a new Irish bill would cause. For the first time in generations Ireland was contented and well governed. Once afflicted by the Union, Irishmen were now its main beneficiaries. It was an irresponsible politician, therefore, who would risk stirring up old animosities for short-term political gain. It bordered on criminal negligence, moreover, when one recalled who the main advocates of Irish Home Rule were. Asquith, it reminded its readers, was not a free agent, but was controlled in this matter by John Redmond, who, in turn, was dependent upon Irish America that had "but one desire." Ulster, therefore, should not be condemned for its stance, but congratulated. Its cause was not treason but loyalty. "Her fight is for the maintenance of the rights her citizens have enjoyed for generations, and which they hope to preserve for their children after them." For these rights Ulster was willing to make any sacrifice, however costly, "and in her struggle she ought to have the sympathy and support of Britons everywhere."[57]

Others emphasised that conceding Ulster's case was not to oppose democracy, but to broaden its scope. If Catholic Ireland was granted the right to self-determination, it was inconsistent to deny that right to Protestant Ulster. While admitting that the possibility of civil war in Ireland was alarming, the *Toronto Star* argued that Ulster "could not rebel if she were not coerced." If coercing Catholic Ireland to accept the status quo was wrong, then coercing Ulster to abandon it was equally wrong. While admitting that the division of Ireland may not be desirable, Britain should allow "the people of Ireland liberty to divide as they please." Place the matter squarely in the hands of the Irish people themselves. "Give them such a measure as will enable them to see how home rule works out. Give them the option of making Ireland one Province or two Provinces. With no

45

coercion, with perfect liberty, the solution will be found."[58]

> Exclusion or division would solve the religious question, as well as it can be solved in this imperfect world. It would establish a Catholic Province like Quebec and a Protestant Province like Ontario. It is true that there would be dissatisfied Catholics in Ulster or the segregated part of Ulster and dissatisfied Protestants in the rest of Ireland. So it is in Ontario and Quebec. We cannot form any sort of government under which there will not be dissatisfied individuals.[59]

It is certainly true that not everyone was won over by the Ulstermen's crusade, or by the logic of their case against inclusion. The *Toronto Globe*, for example, noted that unionists claimed the right "not only of freedom for Ulster Unionists to remain outside the jurisdiction of the Irish Parliament, but also the right to force Ulster Nationalists to remain out."[60] The *Nanaimo Free Press* charged that Carson was evidently an agent of those reactionary forces determined "to hinder the wheels of political freedom" in Great Britain itself.[61] For such men Ulster was not the cause, but the occasion. Others agreed. The *Victoria Daily Times* added that the larger agenda of the unionist leadership was to stop "the tide of democratic progress."[62] Harsh criticism was also directed at the Ulstermen's resolve to resist Home Rule by force. The *Toronto World* noted that it seemed incredulous that in the 20th century parliament was being blackmailed by cavaliers "who advocate rebellion and civil war rather than submission to constitutional procedure."[63] The *Anglican Churchman* was particularly taken aback by the support offered to Carson by prominent British Conservatives such as Bonar Law. Home Rule it conceded "may not be in the interests of Ireland or the Empire" but the behaviour of otherwise responsible politicians was still astonishing. If Bonar Law's words in Belfast meant anything, it concluded, "they meant his sanction and encouragement to open rebellion because of a law to be enacted by the constitutionally elected representatives of the people of Great Britain and Ireland."[64] For the *Victoria Daily Times*, regardless of the merits (or otherwise) of the unionist case against Home Rule, it was completely inappropriate for Canadian officials to be involving themselves in the Irish issue, let alone encouraging open resistance to established authority. When pro-Home Rule resolutions had been introduced into parliament in the past, the *Times* had condemned them as an unwarranted interference in Britain's affairs. In 1914 its position had not changed. "If the Canadian government does its duty," it admonished, "it will sharply rebuke its trade commissioner in Glasgow for his participation in the Orangemen's demonstration." The question of Home Rule for Ireland was a political issue in the United Kingdom and "officials of the Canadian government over there must keep themselves clear of it."[65]

But if there remained a good deal of support for the principle of Home Rule in the media, and criticism of unionist methods of protest, it remained in the editorial columns. Newspaper headlines, and the content of on-the-spot reports on page one were strongly sympathetic to the Ulstermen. The unionist cause had seized the imagination of the day. Writing in 1909, George Denison had lamented that, in years passed, those Canadians who supported Irish Home Rule, and the validity of the Canadian Analogy, had not been challenged with sufficient vigour. On the streets and in the legislatures the cause of Parnell and Redmond had been setting the agenda, noted Denison, despite the fact that Canadians "were not generally favourable to the movement."[66] Other prominent Canadians had also expressed their disappointment at the inability of Canadian 'loyalists' to seize the initiative in the dominion. By 1912, Denison and supporters--whether they were the majority or not--had taken to the streets, parading, demonstrating, organising fund-raisers, and applauding the prospect of Ulstermen taking up arms against the British government.

They had set the agenda to which supporters of Home Rule were now forced to respond. And in the House of Commons, it was the issue of support for Carson, not Redmond, that caught attention. Indeed, after protesting that yet another member, this time a cabinet minister, had been a party to a delegation that had "anything but a peaceful purpose" in presenting a sword to Sir Edward Carson in London on the eve of his departure for Belfast, a member of the opposition accused the government itself of complicity.

> It may be that the hon. gentlemen who form this ministry are not averse to having it known that they strongly sympathise with the gentlemen in the north of Ireland.[67]

The opposition member may very well have been overstating the case, but his assertion in itself underlines the extent to which nationalist fortunes had plummeted within English Canada since 1882. Nationalist fortunes in Canada would decline even further when Catholic Ireland turned away from constitutional agitation in 1917 to give its support to Sinn Fein. This development, and the anti-British rhetoric that its supporters used in Canada, cost it dearly. Most disastrously, however, Sinn Fein's supporters in Canada made the error of transferring their analysis of Ireland's ills to Canada. This, and the political climate existent in post-war Canada, spelled the end of Canada's special relationship with Irish nationalism.

PART TWO

--CHAPTER FOUR--

An Associated Press despatch says that 'President' de Valera was in consultation last week at Plattsburg, N.Y., with fifty Canadian men and women 'said to be sympathetic with his solution of the Irish problem'. His solution is the disruption of the United Kingdom and the British Empire by the setting up of an independent Irish Republic. His method is to try to embroil the United States and the British Empire in war...Canada is a part of the British Empire and would be involved in any complications between Washington and London over the Irish question. Only enemies of this country, whether they live in it or not, would associate themselves with what is in effect a conspiracy against its peace and security.[68]

SINN FEIN AND REVOLUTION

Over the five years that followed the Easter Rising matters rapidly deteriorated in Ireland. The Easter Rebellion, and the crown's clumsy response, had altered Anglo-Irish relations for the worse. This change in mood was made painfully clear to the British after the general election of December 1918. Out of 79 seats taken by nationalists, 73 were taken by members of the republican Sinn Fein party--36 of whom were serving prison terms in English jails. The constitutional Nationalist Party won a total of six seats. Refusing to take their seats at Westminster, the Sinn Fein representatives met in Dublin where they proceeded to establish an Irish parliament (Dail Eireann) and proclaim anew the Irish republic of 1916. The new armed wing of Sinn Fein--the Irish Republican Army(IRA)--immediately set about putting the Dail's claim into effect through a campaign of assassination against the Royal Irish Constabulary, a potent symbol of the crown's authority in Ireland. London's response was

Low – *The Statesman*, 11 June 1921

John Bull Shores Up the Old Order.

to introduce the 'Black and Tans', a paramilitary force resolved to match republican terror with an equally ruthless counter-terror.

The position of the British government in the years under study, therefore, was an unenviable one. It was a position, moreover, made considerably less pleasant by the support that republicans had managed to secure for their cause abroad. In the United States, Irish Americans were unusually active in organising and financing support for the republican cause, particularly after the events of 1916. Among other undertakings, they actively publicised the 'barbarism' of the British executions, promoted anti-British sentiment across the country over a wide spectrum of issues, sponsored speaking tours of prominent republicans, and agitated for Irish recognition at the Versailles Peace Conference. In February of 1919 they organised an Irish Race Convention at Philadelphia, which was enthusiastically attended by politicians, Roman Catholic bishops, and prominent Irish American laypersons. The convention unanimously passed a resolution supporting the right of the Irish people to establish a republican government. In the political arena, the convention's call was matched by the House of Representatives' resolution that Ireland's case be considered at the upcoming Peace Conference. A similar resolution was endorsed by the American Senate, while a semi-official committee of prominent Americans, 'The Committee of One Hundred', conducted a public inquiry, and issued a scathingly critical report of British military operations in Ireland.

In Canada, there also existed those who championed the cause of Irish republicanism. For some, American initiatives on behalf of Ireland were worthy of the highest praise. Not least among those who championed the republican cause were elements within Canada's Irish community and the weekly Roman Catholic press. In February 1920 the Self-Determination League for Ireland was founded in Montreal to champion the cause of an independent Irish republic, and an affiliated newspaper, *The Statesman*, served to keep the nationalist perspective before the Canadian public. In February 1920, more than a year before the American report was released to the public, *The Statesman* had the following to say.

> The Irish Question is a world issue. It has long ago ceased to be a private question between either the English or the Irish. What might have been merely a domestic problem has become an international scandal. As the world had to take notice of the German outrage on Belgium, the Austrian attack on Serbia, the oppression of the Armenians, by the same token the world is concerned in the continued oppression of Ireland. The frustrations of their national life, the agitation, disorder, resentment and brutal waste which English tyranny is responsible for, now concern all of mankind--for freedom is not a private possession...[I]t is the essential right of humanity itself.[69]

Unlike the case in the United States, however, those who championed Sinn Fein and an Irish republic found themselves to be a small and ineffective minority. Public opinion, as expressed in the daily and weekly press, and public demonstrations, was overwhelmingly supportive of Great Britain and implacably hostile to Sinn Fein. No political initiatives were introduced on behalf of Irish nationalism, and *Hansard* records only one reference to Ireland during these years. Politicians, the media, and various organisations, moreover, bitterly denounced American interference in the United Kingdom's internal affairs, and urged parliament to ban American Sinn Fein journals, and sympathisers, from entering Canada. Canada's own advocates of Sinn Fein's position were closely watched by the RCMP from the beginning, and more than a few found themselves in receipt of deportation orders. Unlike the United States, Canada was inhospitable ground for those espousing sympathy or support for Sinn Fein.

The Irish cause was also irreversibly damaged in Canada by its association, in the minds of many, with other 'agitators' who travelled the country after the Great War damning the existing social order. Bolsheviks, anarchists, German agents, and others, were believed to be *everywhere* in 1919, all holding to a common hatred of Great Britain. For many, Sinn Fein and its proponents fell neatly into this category. Most significantly perhaps, the Irish cause was done considerable damage by its proponents' insistence on transferring their evaluation of the Irish Question to the 'Canadian Question'. The bitterness with which British rule was condemned in Ireland was matched by its damnation of 'British rule' in Canada. This digression caused the Self-Determination League considerably in the eyes of the Canadian public.

SELF-INFLICTED WOUNDS

At the most basic level the Canadian defence of British policy in Ireland stemmed from the belief that whatever measures Great Britain was using to subdue the IRA, they were justifiable given the atrocities regularly perpetrated by the IRA itself. Many took offence at the suggestion of Irish Americans, and American politicians in their apparent haste to secure the Irish ballot, to publicise British paramilitary tactics in Ireland without placing them in context. In April of 1921 the *Hamilton Spectator* was generally representative in its contempt for the American commission into British military activities in Ireland.

> The report of the 'committee of one hundred', which pretended to investigate conditions in Ireland, is a document which cannot be taken seriously. It is a mere rehash of such prejudiced accounts of British 'misdeeds' as have been distributed ad nauseam by Irish republican sympathisers in recent times....In its lurid presentation of the policy of reprisals by the British, no account whatever is taken of the brutal and cowardly acts of the Sinn Feiners which made that policy necessary.[70]

With few exceptions the entire English-Canadian press expressed similar sentiments. If Britain was using coercive measures in Ireland today, concluded the *Calgary Herald*, "the fault lies with the Irish themselves."[71] "Ireland's greatest enemies," agreed the *Charlottetown Examiner*, "...have been those of her own household."[72] With regard to the well-publicised excesses of the Black and Tans, the English-Canadian press again remained unmoved. The *Canadian Churchman*, for example, argued that, as IRA provocation was often great, it was unfortunate, but inevitable, that "men brutalised by war and maddened by drink should get out of control when they see their comrades fall from the bullets of cowardly assassins."[73] Other papers backed up this argument with the assertion that British honour was at stake in Ireland. The *Guelph Evening Mercury*, for example, argued that, after the long and bloody struggle in Europe, Britain would appear ridiculous should it now succumb to "a few hundred men who shoot policemen from ambush."[74]

Few English Canadians conceded, moreover, that there was any substance to the charge of criminal mismanagement of Irish affairs against the British government. Noone denied that, in generations passed, Irish Catholics had been woefully treated by the British government, and that reparations had been due. Even here, however, it was acknowledged that British policy had often been directed by geo-political considerations, and legitimate concerns about Irish collaboration with the crown's enemies in time of war.[75] As for reparations, all were in agreement that great social reform initiatives had, long ago, transformed Ireland from a land of impoverishment to one of unprecedented prosperity. In February of 1920 a delegation of prominent Ulster unionists spoke to large and enthusiastic audiences throughout Toronto on this very theme, reassuring those who held to this viewpoint, and converting many who previously had not. The *Toronto Globe*, for example, which had been notable in pre-war years for its advocacy of Irish Home Rule, reported on the delegation's speeches in glowing terms. [76] All the talk of British misrule in Ireland, went the general consensus, was mere propaganda and believable only to minds prejudiced to the truth. "[I]t does seem strange," concluded the *Christian Guardian*, "that while Scotland, and Wales, and Ulster, and Canada are under the British Government and are not complaining at all, Roman Catholic Ireland is filling the world with its wails."[77] Despite the dramatic improvement in Irish life over the past half-century, noted *Maclean's* magazine, an irrational hatred of England remained "as a hand before their eyes."[78]

'THE VARIOUS FORCES OF UNREST'

With virtually one voice English-Canadian opinion makers condemned American support for an all-Ireland Irish republic. This option, it argued, was unreasonable and unworkable, and American advocacy of it was a grave offence to its wartime ally. "Britain's courtesy and patience," noted the *Toronto Globe*, "have been grossly abused by demagogues of the United States."[79] "For the United States to interfere in a question involving the integrity of the United Kingdom," concurred the *Presbyterian Witness*, was "perilously near an unfriendly act."[80] Particularly annoying to Canadians was the hypocrisy they believed to be lurking behind American support for Irish independence. Had the American government allowed the southern Confederacy to secede from the Union? Of course not. And it had put the American people through the fiercest and bitterest of wars to prevent it.[81] Wherein then lay American judgement on Great Britain in its resolve to maintain the integrity of the United Kingdom? Was the republic's own record of civil rights without blemish? Certainly not. And every reading suggested that Britain was considerably more tolerant of its internal enemies than the United States had been of its own. "[W]here but in London, England," asked the *Presbyterian Witness*, "would the Government have allowed a rebel flag to be carried through the streets of its greatest city, as happened at Mayor MacSwiney's funeral?"[82] Could the Confederate flag have been carried through New York? Would Washington, moreover, have tolerated, even for a moment, a hostile nation sitting immediately off its own coast? Of course not. Wherein then lay the justification of the American critique of Great Britain's right to self-preservation?

The universal consensus was that a number of factors had contributed to American interference in the United Kingdom's internal affairs. Foremost among these were the anglophobic opinions of certain American newspapers (particularly those controlled by William Hearst),[83] and the unprincipled scramble after the Irish ballot by politicians anxious to secure reelection.[84] For others, however, the hostile new atmosphere was being contrived by those in high places--be it Rome, Berlin or Moscow--and Sinn Fein was its unwitting tool. As early as December 1918 the *Toronto World* stated that it was the purpose

> ...of reactionaries of every description who worship autocracy and despotism in one form or another, Bolshevistic, imperialistic, dynastic, socialistic or spiritualistic, to do what is possible to breed misunderstandings and to foster debate between the two sections of the English-speaking peoples.[85]

In May of 1920 this sentiment was again expressed in a long contributed article to the *Orange Sentinel*. After listing the many socio-economic ills that had befallen Canada since the war's end the author concluded that it was manifest "that the various forces of unrest are well organised." If the truth could be known he continued, it would be disclosed "that Sinn Fein...has its influence in these movements; that all these and other movements, known and unknown, bear evidence of Sinn Fein."[86] Such sentiments were not those of a few overly-active imaginations, however, but could be found at all levels of society. In a speech before the prestigious Empire Club of Canada in 1920, an American-born professor at the University of Toronto drove this theme home (albeit with a new twist) to an enthusiastic audience. "De Valera in himself," he insisted, "is only an incident, only a symptom, only one of those evidences that, far underneath the surface, great forces are at work and are using all the De Valeras in the world as their tools--De Valera is nothing; he is the fictitious President of a fictitious republic."[87] Among those most active were the German government, seeking to avenge its defeat by encouraging dissent between America and Britain, and international Bolshevism anxious to further the cause of Marx and Lenin.[88] The English-speaking people, if they were to resist the onslaught, had to stand as one.

While not discounting the involvement of Bolsheviks and agents of the Kaiser, others saw a much older adversary at work--Roman Catholicism. Whether or not one imagined that Rome was the driving force behind Sinn Fein, there was a concerted belief that the Catholic hierarchy was, at the very least, consistently turning a blind eye to murder. Some editorials were more diplomatic in their wording than others. The *Calgary Herald* of December 1919 noted that "in other lands the Roman Catholic Church had in times past exercised important influence over its people, leading them into an attitude of agreement with law and order, thus making the duties of those in authority easy." It seemed inconceivable that, in the most Catholic of countries, the Church suddenly found itself without influence.[89] The extent of the hierarchy's silence on the matter of violence was proof to many that, however

Gracey – *Montreal Daily Star*, 27 September 1920

craftily it manufactured its international image, Rome did not change. "No voice is seriously raised in protest," noted the *Canadian Churchman*. "No expression of horror at the bloody carnival of cowards operating in the dark."[90] For the Methodist *Christian Guardian*, regardless of the role played by the Catholic hierarchy in the unrest, it was further proof of the incompatibility of Roman Catholicism with British loyalty. In December of 1920 it stated the following.

> The British Empire, mighty beyond precedent, stands as the greatest imperial exponent of Protestantism in the world, and with the addition of the United States, represents the great evangelising and colonising world-forces of Protestantism...And this is one reason why the Sinn Feiners hate Britain, and would gladly compass her fall. To them it is not alone a struggle for a free Ireland, but a war against the greatest heretic Empire the world ever saw.[91]

SINN FEIN AND FENIANISM

Another significant factor that had worked against Sinn Fein in Canada was that of historical memory--particularly that of the Fenian Raids of the late 1860s. Although one has to look between the lines to see it, it was there. Fenianism's place in the English-Canadian psyche was sufficiently pervasive, it didn't warrant being discussed. Every Canadian school child was aware that, between 1866-70, while US officials turned a blind eye, or wished the intruders well, armed bands of Irish Americans had marched into Canada. Having returned from service in the Union Army to find that no employment awaited them, several thousand had resolved on seizing British America as a bargaining chip in their ongoing war with Great Britain. Although the raids were little more than a regular nuisance, Canadians quickly came to associate militant Irish republicanism not only with hatred of England, but with questionable loyalty to Canada. Between 1918 and 1922 few Canadians would have been oblivious to these echoes from the past.

It was to Sinn Fein's detriment that Canadians, like Irishmen, had memories--and few would have been unaware that Sinn Fein claimed to carry forward the Fenian standard of implacable resistance to everything British. Even the very name of Sinn Fein's ally must have rung familiar in the ears of many. The letters 'IRA' had, after all, been emblazoned on the banners that American Fenians carried aloft when they crossed into Canada. And it was a Fenian who shot and killed D'Arcy McGee on an Ottawa street in 1868, one year after the confederation of Britain's North American colonies that he had helped bring about. For many D'Arcy McGee had been a symbol of Canada's promise. A symbol of the merits of non-revolutionary nationalism. The most articulate advocate of the Canadian dream. His death, therefore, was a great shock to most Canadians, and even the few militant Irish *emigre* newspapers that there were, such as Ontario's *Irish Canadian*, moved with remarkable speed to distance themselves from the act. But the *Irish Canadian*, and the handful of other small publications that shared their political outlook, had already done their share in alienating Fenianism within Canada. Their affection for Irish republicanism in the past had, after all, gone hand in hand with that other cause they espoused--the annexation of Canada by the United States of America. Fenianism in Canada, therefore, had always signified not only hatred of Great Britain, but disloyalty to Canada.

The cause of Irish republicanism was irreversibly damaged in Canada, moreover, by the fervency with which its advocates continued to condemn Great Britain and everything British after 1918. As already noted, the Self-Determination League for Ireland in Canada was the most outspoken critic of British policy in Ireland. Addressing a Self-Determination League meeting in Montreal a prominent French Canadian member of that body, Armand Lavergne, had condemned England as, without doubt, history's "greatest murderer of small nations."[92] England's administration of

Ireland, argued the *Statesman*, was "a diabolical tyranny."[93] The entire imperial structure, added Toronto's *Catholic Register*, was a "hideous scandal," a "family compact" of the privileged, the bigoted, and the powerful.[94] It was inevitable that such bitter criticism of Great Britain should provoke a hostile response within English Canada.

It needs emphasising, moreover, that, despite Canada's increased autonomy within the commonwealth/empire, post-war Canadian nationalism remained a *British* nationalism, and most English Canadians continued to maintain a deep affection for empire. While significant differences existed regarding the exact constitutional link to the British government (if not the crown), and the ideal organisational structure of the British empire, few desired to break that link. It was with predictable consequences, therefore, that the Self-Determination League transferred its analysis of Ireland's ills to those of Canada. Titles such as 'Our Imperialized School System', 'Monarchy or Republic?', and 'Is Canada Independent?' headed articles that assaulted every aspect of Canada's Britishness, not least Canada's membership in the British empire. And not only did the League champion the extension of French language rights outside the Province of Quebec, not only did it openly question the motive of Great Britain's (and hence Canada's) entry into the Great War, but openly expressed contempt for those Canadians who demanded undying fealty from their Irish neighbours. It was indecent, argued the *Statesman*, to ask the Irish in Canada to honour a flag "stained with the blood of their people" and to declare loyalty to a crown that, in their homeland, rested upon "the might of armed assassins."[95] British rule in Ireland was no different from German rule in Belgium! That Canadians could not see this was due to "that hateful imperial delusion...the worship of Wotan because he flies the Union Jack instead of the Iron Cross."[96]

The response of the English-Canadian press to such criticism was unforgiving. Canada, argued the *Kingston British Whig*, ought to use the full weight of the law against such people who "condemn the British flag while content to live and grow prosperous under its protection."[97] Public outrage was also expressed in a variety of other forums. In May of 1921, for example, the Winnipeg Kiwanis Club had refused to hear Lindsay Crawford any further after he made reference to Englishmen as 'foreigners'; that December, a Fredericton meeting was broken up by returned soldiers; and the following week, a meeting at Moncton, New Brunswick, had concluded with the crowd forcing Crawford to kiss the Union Jack.[98] While some meetings occasionally concluded without incident, at others police escorts were required to ensure the safety of the audience upon their release from the hall. On at least one occasion, at Vancouver, a hostile crowd outside the auditorium was estimated at over two thousand.[99]

--CHAPTER FIVE--

THE IRISH FREE STATE (1921-25)

While the IRA and the British Army battled each other on the ground, London was again undertaking political initiatives aimed at resolving the Irish Question. In 1920 the British government introduced a fourth Home Rule bill. Unlike the previous three, however, it provided for a separate parliament for the six north-eastern counties of Ulster. Unionist insistence that they would forcibly resist Dublin rule, combined with London's sense of indebtedness for unionist support during the war, had made partition inevitable. As noted earlier, however, partition was the first choice of no faction anywhere in Ireland or Great Britain. Even unionists had embraced it as a last resort. With the swing towards Sinn Fein in southern Ireland after 1917, however, Ulster unionists became convinced that the two communities in Ireland were destined to different futures, separate and apart. Unionists, therefore, quickly set out to make Northern Ireland an established fact. Several factors determined that they would deem this to be a credible option. Unlike southern unionists, northerners were predominantly Presbyterian in faith, with virtually no adherents outside Ulster. And unlike the Church of Ireland, Irish Presbyterianism was headquartered in Belfast, not Dublin. Ulster unionists were convinced, therefore, that they had nothing to lose by going it alone. But few were desirous of setting up a separate *parliament* in Ulster. For half a century they had espoused the constitutional *status quo*, and campaigned against a separate legislature for Ireland. Their stated desire was to remain within the Union with a status equal to that of Scotland, England and Wales. If nothing else, to now request their own 'Home Rule' legislature would be immensely embarrassing. Noone wanted it and noone asked for it.

The Government of Ireland Act (1920), however, did just that. Besides establishing the border between North and South, it set up two legislatures in Ireland: one in Dublin to govern the southern 26 counties, and another in Belfast to govern the remaining six. It was further legislated that, should it be willed by a majority vote in each legislature, the border would be erased and the two parliaments merged into one. The terms and conditions, within limit, were for the Irish to decide. Ulster unionists reluctantly embraced the parliament imposed on them, while, in the South, Sinn Fein held the entire initiative in contempt. The southern electorate had given them a mandate to establish a republic and nothing less, a mandate subsequently renewed in the elections to the new Home Rule parliament. Sinn Fein won a landslide in the South, set up their own republican parliament, and informed the British that their latest initiative was too little too late. The Irish conflict was about Ireland's absolute right to absolute freedom, nothing less. The war was still on, and, well financed by American sympathisers, the IRA stepped up its armed campaign against the security forces.

In Canada the settlement was generally considered to be reasonable. While some commentators suggested that some sort of dominion status for nationalist Ireland would have been more realistic, others remained adamant that Home Rule within the United Kingdom was the most London could safely grant. Even the *Toronto Globe*, one of the most enthusiastic advocates of Home Rule in the pre-war years, argued against any further concessions. The partition of Ireland was also accepted as a reflection of existing realities. Back in Ireland, however, nationalists viewed things very differently, and in the May 1921 elections to the 'Home Rule' parliament, Sinn Fein was handed 124 out of 128 seats. Tired of conflict and engrossed by social ills closer to home, the British government now offered southern Ireland dominion status. Southern Ireland's status, as outlined in the Anglo-Irish Treaty of 1922, was to be 'that of Canada'. Articles 2 and 3 read as follows.

    2. Subject to the provisions hereinafter
       set out the position of the Irish Free

State in relation to the Imperial Parliament and Government and otherwise shall be that of the Dominion of Canada, and the law, practice and constitutional usage governing the relationship of the Crown or the representative of the Crown and of the Imperial Parliament to the Dominion of Canada shall govern their relationship to the Irish Free State.

3. The representative of the Crown in Ireland shall be appointed in like manner as the Governor-General of Canada and in accordance with the practice observed in the making of such appointments.[100]

Britain insisted that this was its final offer, an assertion that was reluctantly accepted by the Sinn Fein delegation, led by Michael Collins, which signed the treaty in London. In Canada response to the Treaty was mixed. Many observers held to the conviction that dominion status would inevitably mean a declaration of independence and an Irish republic antagonistic to England the moment Sinn Fein attained legislative power.[101] Lloyd George, they argued, was altogether too anxious to secure peace in the short-term, regardless of what it might hold for future generations. Others saw things very differently, being rather taken by the novelty of having an Irish dominion based on the experience of Canada. It was flattering. It was also more likely to win over moderate nationalists than a mere measure of Home Rule. As such it would further contribute to stability in Ireland, and make the reunification of the island more likely. The occasional commentator insisted that it was now time for Ulster to take a courageous step forward and join in the building of the Irish Free State. While the negotiations between Sinn Fein and London were in progress a major Protestant weekly insisted that, if, "in this great crisis of the empire, the north of Ireland should stand out obstinately against the present proposal, much of the sympathy which has hitherto been given to Ulster would undoubtedly be withdrawn, and its case...seriously jeopardized."[102]

DISPARATE DOMINIONS

But while the novelty of having the Free State's status defined as "that of the Dominion of Canada" had romantic appeal for some, most acknowledged it as simply that, romanticism. It was painfully obvious to most Canadian observers that the history of Ireland, and the attitude of the Irish majority to the British link and empire, was *not* that of Canada. It had been mere fantasy to imagine that it was, or could ever have been. Several factors, both long and short term, had marked Ireland out as different. The most immediate factor was that southern Ireland had just attained dominion status as a result of republican insurrection. As an article in the *Canadian Historical Review* observed, "Ireland's position as a Dominion rests upon a treaty between representatives of Britain and representatives of Sinn Fein. There is no parallel to this in the past relations of Canada and Britain, nor indeed is there another parallel in the history of the Empire...Dominion status in Ireland has been the result of a revolution. In Canada, as elsewhere in the Commonwealth, liberty came with the slow growth of national manhood."[103]

Most were aware, moreover, that dominion status had been imposed on the Irish by the British government. Canadians were also aware that even *Cumann na nGaedheal*, the voice of Ireland's pro-Treaty faction, was less than enthusiastic about dominion status. *Cumann na nGaedheal* was a republican party, whose ranks consisted of, among others, former IRA men. It differed from anti-Treaty elements over means not ends. Violence would get nothing more from the British. To continue the guerrilla campaign would be irresponsible and counter-productive. The republic *would* be attained, but in a gradualist, Fabian-like process. Michael Collins' himself had insisted that the Treaty was useless if it did not serve as a 'stepping stone' to the republic

IN SEARCH OF HARMONY

Hard-working harp-tuner: — Whew!—But I'll get it going yet!

Montreal Daily Star, 17 March 1920

proclaimed in 1916. It was not a settlement in itself. "Who can tell," asked the *Daily Mail and Empire*, "what the future of the Irish Free State will be?."

Michael Collins himself continues to refer to England as a 'foreign nation', notwithstanding the clause in the oath he helped to frame, which lays stress upon 'common citizenship of Ireland with England', and has proclaimed with stentorian tones in the Dail that he

> does not regard the treaty as a final
> settlement...These are incontrovertible,
> cold facts, which must be faced, and
> are of themselves ominous of coming
> trouble.

And, as the *Mail and Empire* pointed out, these facts only applied to those *favouring* acceptance. Those opposed to acceptance continued to make no secret of their hostility to any British link whatsoever. "It is to them that the worst Irish-American and Bolshevist elements look to keep alive and further in Ireland the great conspiracy for the destruction of our Empire."[104]

Many Canadian observers were made more apprehensive yet when the Anglo-Irish Treaty, considered a generous and courageous measure on behalf of the British government, passed the Dail by a mere six votes.[105] When the anti-Treaty forces insisted that they would not accept the verdict of the Dail, that it was a betrayal of the republican cause, the stage, as many had feared, was set for civil war. When anti-Treaty forces seized the Four Courts in Dublin and refused the government's ultimatum to surrender, it was besieged. Violence spread and before the anti-Treaty forces finally surrendered, hundreds of former comrades lay dead. As the civil war progressed, however, many Canadian observers came to admire the resolve and determination of the Dublin government in its campaign against the rebels. Perhaps there was hope yet. Perhaps political opinion, and public opinion, would come around to the idea of dominion status.

For many others, however, admiration for Dublin's resolve in the civil war was partially offset by apprehension about the Free State's approach to relations with Northern Ireland. Rather than attempting to woo unionists, it appeared that Dublin had resolved on *coercing* them. The most blatant evidence of this seemed to be its appetite for reopening the boundary question, ostensibly settled by the Government of Ireland Act in 1920. That act had stipulated that no part of Northern Ireland could secede to the South without the consent of the Ulster government. Dublin's repeated claim, however, that it was unjust for Northern Ireland to hold those parts of Ulster with a Catholic majority finally forced London to concede a boundary commission to see which parts of Northern Ireland should be ceded to the Free State. To most Canadian commentators this was a dangerous folly. Not only did it break faith with the Government of Ireland Act, it was a completely transparent attempt to reduce Northern Ireland's territory with the goal of weakening its chances of surviving as a separate entity. The grave danger of this policy was that it was not likely to work, and certain to increase the enmity between North and South. The timing was also remarkably poor, given that feelings in Ulster were already agitated by the ongoing IRA campaign against the Northern government, a campaign which many unionists believed to have the blessing of Dublin. An article in the *Dalhousie Review* had the following to say on the matter.

> The difference in race, religion, traditions and ideals, not to mention occupations and interests, makes complete union between Ulster and the South impossible; but that a working arrangement between North and South, which will for most purposes abolish the boundaries between the two, will-- if good government continues in the South--come about before many years, is the opinion of most intelligent observers. It will be a terrible calamity if that end is defeated by an exasperating struggle over those boundaries which, if southern Ireland only tries to obey Lord Carson's counsel and 'win Ulster', will soon cease to exist.[106]

By the time the Boundary Commission finally issued its report in 1925 its credibility was already greatly diminished. Ulster was resolved to concede 'not an inch', and had embraced as its new logo 'What We Have We Hold'. When the commissioners reported that, on the basis of consent, that parts of the Free State, notably parts of Donegal, would have to be ceded to Northern Ireland, even Dublin lost interest in the report.

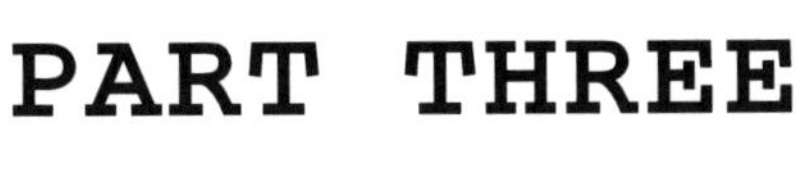

PART THREE

--CHAPTER SIX--

IRISH CANADIANS AND IRELAND (1867-1925)

Before moving on to examine Canadian involvement in Irish developments in the post-1925 era, it is necessary to take a closer look at Canada's Irish Catholic community and its response to Irish developments up to 1925. Canada's Irish Catholics, to put it mildly, occupied a unique and anomalous place within the dominion. This was manifestly apparent with the polarisation of positions on the Irish Question after the Great War. Although a majority of Ireland's Catholics had transferred their support away from constitutional nationalism and toward militant republicanism, it was difficult for Canada's Irish to support such a move. Some had become totally assimilated into Canadian society by this time, and didn't feel compelled to express a hard position on the issue one way or another. Others, however, had not abandoned their Irish identity, and responded with bitter attacks against the British government's policy and threw their support behind the Self-Determination League. Perhaps a majority, however, found themselves in the extremely uncomfortable position of having to choose between two deeply felt allegiances--their loyalty to the British crown and their affinity with their co-religionists in Ireland. These conflicting loyalties made the conflict in Ireland a most distressing one indeed. Most were glad to see it resolved, as much for their own sakes as for the sakes of those in Ireland itself.

Unlike their neighbours in the United States, Irish Catholics in Canada had rarely embraced the extremist brand of Irish nationalism. In fact, their development as a community in Canada stood in stark contrast to that of Irish America. Several long-term factors had determined that this would be so. Irish Catholics had arrived in Canada in considerably smaller numbers than in the United States, and settled almost evenly in city and countryside, avoiding the physical and psychological ghettoization evident in Boston and New York. They had also arrived in a country that, unlike the United States, had a significant European Catholic community as one of its founding peoples. They became citizens of a country that, unlike the United States, possessed no revolutionary tradition. They shared their new land with a majority population that was positively enthusiastic about its Britishness and that looked upon republicanism, even as a concept, with deep suspicion. They had arrived in a land where the French minority, while less enthusiastic about matters imperial than their British neighbours, decidedly preferred the British connection to the alternative: incorporation into the ultra-Protestant United States. This French Catholic community, moreover, despite long-standing grievances against the majority population, also inherited no revolutionary tradition. All these factors contributed to the making of an Irish-Canadian community remarkably different from that of the United States.

Other factors also played their part. As mentioned earlier, Canada, in the 1860s, had been subjected to a number of invasions by American Fenians. As a result Fenianism came to represent questionable loyalties, both to Great Britain and to Canada. From that time on Canada's Irish communities worked to put distance between themselves and Irish America. All these factors, aligned to everyday concerns, physical distance, and the passage of time, served to weaken the emotional link with Ireland.

This chapter will undertake to do three things. First it will further explore the cultural development of the Irish Catholic community in British North America. Secondly it will look at the emergence of the Irish pro-Home Rule lobby in Canada after 1870, and its varying fortunes. Thirdly, it will examine the response of Irish Canadians to the polarisation of opinion in Ireland and Canada alike after the Great War.

D'ARCY MCGEE AND IRISH-CANADIANISM

No discussion of the cultural development of Canada's Irish community can progress very far without the conversation turning to Thomas D'Arcy

McGee. D'Arcy McGee is most frequently cited as the exemplar of Irish Catholicism's reconciliation with the British empire. He was, however, a most unlikely candidate for such notoriety. In his youth D'Arcy McGee had been a militant nationalist, dedicated to the removal of English writ from Irish soil by force of arms. As had so frequently been the case in the past, however, the attempted revolution failed and McGee accompanied another generation of Irish nationalists into American exile. With many of his compatriots, however, he expected this departure to be but a temporary setback on the road to freedom; from abroad he and his fellows would organise and agitate until Ireland was finally emancipated from English yoke, taking its rightful place among free nations. Regardless of what others may have found, or claimed to have found, however, the American republic across the Atlantic was not what McGee dreamt it might have been. Rather than finding the idealised land of opportunity and freedom, he had found a society with deeply entrenched cultural and racial biases, and an unwelcome Irish community crowded into the urban slums of Boston and New York. If de Tocqueville "were now to go over the same ground, familiar as he was with it formerly," McGee later wrote to a friend, "much of his work would probably be rewritten." The land of welcome and equality, so popularised in Cork and Kerry, and the hills of Donegal, was a myth. Somewhat ironically, he believed this fact to be demonstrated by the dogged persistence of Irish nationalist sentiment in America.

> This very Fenian organisation in the United States, what does it really prove, but that the Irish are still an alien population, camped but not settled in America, with foreign hopes and aspirations unshared by the people among whom they live? If their new country was their true country, would they find time and money to spare in the construction of imaginary Republics beyond seas?[107]

His disillusionment with republican government in general, and the American experiment in particular, was already well advanced when he accepted the offer of Montreal's Irish community in 1857 to help establish an Irish press in that city. Arriving in Canada he came to the conclusion that Irishmen could indeed live contentedly within a British constitutional framework, and concluded that constitutional monarchy aligned with responsible government were preferable to the political uncertainties and excessive democracy of an experimental republic. Canada, he now concluded, was the ideal society to which Ireland ought to aspire. Having made peace with the Catholic Church, with which he had parted company over the means whereby Ireland's ills should be addressed, McGee abandoned his old philosophy, and emerged as perhaps the most eloquent proponent of Canadian confederation and the forging of a new national identity.

Not only did he come to see Canada, and not the United States, as the model and ideal to which Ireland ought to aspire, but insisted that the Irish get on with their lives in their new land. Old World grievances could play no constructive part in the building of the New. Speaking in Montreal in 1863 before a gathering of fellow expatriates, he stated the following.

> The Irish have no grievance in Canada. Have you any state Church here, or landed aristocracy to turn out the peasant upon the highway by summary ejectment? Then if you have no complaint, is it not your duty, as it is that of all other nationalities, to stand by the government and give the highest practical proof possible that an Irishman well governed becomes one of the best subjects of the law and the sovereign?[108]

McGee combated the spread of Fenianism in Canada and advised others to oppose Fenians in their own communities. He not only encouraged Irish Canadians to remove Fenian sympathisers from positions of authority within their organisations, but encouraged the government to appoint an agent to infiltrate the parent organisation in the United States. Irishmen, he admonished, "should never forget that they now live and act in a land of the fullest religious and civil liberty."[109] If anyone wanted to help the Irish in Ireland, insisted McGee, they could do so by providing them, and the British government, with an example of how Ireland's political and social woes might be rectified.

Yet it is unquestionably true that what D'Arcy McGee was asking of Irish Catholics in Canada was a troubling thing, and many responded to his admonitions with open hostility. He was asking them to shelve their pasts, and their deepest feelings, and to embrace British North America as their own, with all of the uncomfortable psychological adjustment which that entailed. While some merely dismissed McGee's vision as unreasonable, others denounced him as an opportunist, a traitor to Ireland, and in 1868, one year after the enactment of the Canadian confederation he had helped bring about, he was felled by an assassin in Ottawa.

McGee, however, had not worked alone. In his efforts to reconcile the Irish to living in a British country, he had the support of his church. Outside of Quebec the Roman Catholic Church was essentially an Irish church, and the hierarchy actively campaigned to redirect the interest of its adherents from Irish to Canadian affairs, and from matters political to matters confessional. There were several reasons for this, not least of which was the church's desire to maintain control over its adherents by warding off any challenge to its authority by lay nationalist organisations. One means of achieving this end was to gradually redefine Irishness in terms of religious devotion rather than race or ethnicity. It was also in part, no doubt, out of a concern not to unnecessarily aggravate the country's Protestant majority. As the hierarchy was fully aware, it took little to convince the country's Orangemen, numerous and influential, that Irish Catholics were inherently disloyal.

76

There is also plenty of evidence that the work of McGee and colleagues had paid off. When, two years after McGee's death, there emerged a new Fenian threat along Canada's border the *Canadian Freeman* noted the following.

> They say they want to wound England and free Ireland by attacking Canada...Let us see what this involves. Canada, as everyone knows, who is at all acquainted with our system of government, is *virtually* independent of England. The people are contented, prosperous and well governed. We enact our own laws, impose our own taxes, spend our money just as we please, without any interference on the part of the mother country. No class or creed has reasonable ground for complaint...Among the inhabitants of the new Dominion, there are several hundred thousands of the countrymen and co-religionists of 'General' O'Neill and his horde, who participate in all the advantages that we have enumerated.[110]

Two years previous, shortly after McGee's death, the *Irish Canadian* in an article entitled "Give Ireland What Canada Has," claimed that the Irish in Canada enjoyed "blissful peace and happiness," and expressed a preference for Canada's constitutional standing over that of the United States with its "disjointed and dislocated political institutions." The Irish in Canada, it concluded, were proof that freedom makes a people "happy, prosperous and loyal."[111] At a gathering of the Irish National League in Toronto in March of 1886, the League's spokesman praised Canada as "..the land of freedom, of religious liberty and federal government."[112]

This same attachment to Canada and the crown was again apparent many years later when the Great War commenced and the Canadian government called on Canadians to rally to the standard. Irish Canadians did so, and many were highly critical of those in French-speaking, and Roman Catholic, Quebec, who appeared to be failing the cause. And unlike the case in the United States there was no Irish lobby against participation in 'England's' war. When American bodies expressed such sentiments Irish Canadians responded with disapproval. No organisation in America was more hostile towards Great Britain than the Ancient Order of Hibernians, an organisation which also had several Canadian chapters. The American body's journal, the *National Hibernian*, for example, had stated its position on the war as early as August 1914. What reason, it asked, had Ireland to hate Germany? "Germany has never done her any harm. Germany has not ravaged or plundered her century after century. Germany has not crippled her resources and driven her people into exile." England had! There was only one position, therefore, that any self-respecting Irishman could take on the war. "Now, as ever," concluded the *Hibernian*, "England's difficulty is Ireland's opportunity." But far from endorsing such sentiments, Canadian Hibernians, across the entire country, expressed outrage that the American body would express such sentiments when their Canadian affiliate was preparing for war. Many chapters announced a long-term dissatisfaction with their American connection, and announced their intentions to secede. Others announced that they were commencing a campaign to have the *National Hibernian* banned as "hostile propaganda" from entering Canada.[113] Who did these people think they were, assuming Canadian Hibernians would agree with such sentiments? Other persons and publications in Canada expressed similar sentiments publicly. "Britain's troubles are our troubles," insisted Toronto's Archbishop, "Britain's shield our safety." "Germany is our enemy," agreed the *Catholic Register*, "and we must do all we can to conquer her."[114] "We as Canadians," it stated in the weeks ahead, "are Britishers to the core."[115]

Not quite. In an overwhelmingly Anglo-Protestant Canada they were still a very visible minority. The crown was Protestant, anti-Catholicism was a vital component of the predominant culture, and the large and influential Orange element never failed to remind them of their 'otherness'. Their very names, moreover, were daily reminders of their ethnic origins. In short, being Irish Canadian was the source of much internal conflict. This was not true of all, but it was of considerable numbers. And it cannot be denied that, on occasion, loud declarations of loyalty to the British connection were prompted less by conviction, and more by concern about the suspicions of the majority population. In 1870, for example, in the wake of renewed Fenian threats along the Canadian frontier, one Irish representative wrote to the governor general of the day stating his community's contempt for "these Fenian marauders," assuring him that "Irishmen of all creeds and parties in Canada are now a unit in respect of their loyalty and devotion to [the] British connection."[116] This was not exactly true. It had been but two years since a Canadian Fenian had assassinated D'Arcy McGee, and the *Irish Canadian*--a journal which, occasional expressions of loyalty aside, was not afraid to express republican and pro-Fenian sentiments when it felt so inclined--would remain in circulation for another twenty-two years. And even after the emergence of journals openly dedicated to Catholic, as opposed to Irish Catholic, interests in the dominion, a certain uneasiness with the British fact remained. Certain phrases, such as 'British connection', frequently appeared in Irish writings on the subject without any attempt at definition. When definitions were offered, they occasionally must have prompted the raising of an imperial eyebrow. Ireland, announced the *Irish Canadian* in 1868, must follow the example of Canada, becoming "a free nation and a great people...bearing but a nominal friendship to England."[117]

A similar use of words was also detectable decades later when the *Catholic Register* stated that "...England's Empire has countless advantages."[118] Few Anglo-Protestant Canadians would have referred to the British empire--an empire that was increasingly their own--as 'England's'. When commenting on Irish developments as late as 1912-14, moreover, Irish Canadians did not express their support of Home Rule in quite the same manner as did other Canadian proponents of the Irish cause. The Catholic press, for example, still reflected a notable absence of what other Canadians would have termed imperial sentiment. It also suggested that much of the old Anglophobia had remained with many within Canada's Irish communities. On 26 March 1914 the *Catholic Record* noted the following.

> England has abolished Ireland's Parliament in 1800, and since then tried to rule Ireland from London, and she has made an egregrious failure of it. England's rule in Ireland has been a failure, and an egregrious failure from every point of view. Was it not time then that she should acknowledge this, and give to Irishmen what she had given so freely to other parts of the Empire--to Australia, to Canada, to South Africa.[119]

"In the meagre measure of self-government which Ireland trusts soon to gain," added the *Catholic Register*, "an advance, at least, will have been made to the goal of ultimate freedom--freedom for all classes and creeds of Irishmen--when that day dawns for Ireland amidst the paean of praise which will go up from a liberated people." And on 16 March 1914, before twenty-five hundred people assembled in Toronto's Massey Hall for a St. Patrick's Day concert, A.T. Hernon, Canadian President of the Ancient Order of Hibernians, stated that "the great God created Ireland an island, isolated and alone, and He in His wisdom decreed her to be a nation."[120] A liberated people? Isolated and alone? Such statements surely suggest a less enthusiastic approach to the collectivist imperial structure to which Canada, as a British nation, belonged than would be offered by Anglo-Protestant proponents of Home Rule.

This gulf was made more blatantly obvious in the months following the Easter Rebellion of 1916, when two thousand nationalists had seized the centre of Dublin and proclaimed an Irish republic. At this time the conflicting loyalties--as Canadian citizens and as Irish Catholic expatriates--were most notable. Although it had initially condemned the rebellion as "utterly unjustified and unjustifiable"[121] and acknowledged that, in time of war, Britain had no alternative but to forcibly quell the uprising, once the executions of the rebel leaders began the *Register's* tone went from resentment to open hostility. For its part the Protestant and secular presses had attempted to justify the executions on a number of grounds. The *Globe*, for example, had insisted that regardless of the political wisdom of the executions, the rebels were "unquestionably guilty of treason and subject to all the penalties that treason entails."[122] In sharp contrast, however, the *Register* began its coverage by noting the disparity in how Britain had dealt with Ireland's *two* rebellious communities. There was a clear 'cause and effect' dynamic at work in Irish developments that the British government, blinded by cultural insensitivity, had clearly overlooked. As the *Register* saw it the Dublin disturbances were a natural result of the Ulster Volunteers' threat to use violence to prevent the implementation of Home Rule in 1912, a move that had inspired the founding of the nationalist Irish Volunteers. The Irish troubles, therefore, were directly caused by "the criminally treasonable conduct of Sir Edward Carson and his associates in preparing and arming for forcible resistance to the law." The punishment "meted out to that arch-traitor was the appointment to a seat in the King's Privy Council." By that act, it asserted, "a premium was put upon treason and armed resistance to lawful authority...But for Carsonist treason there would not have been one unlawfully armed man in Ireland."[123] If Anglo-Protestant critics of Ulster unionists had forgiven Carson's pre-war indiscretions, Irish-Catholic Canadians had not.

From this initial commentary the *Register's* language became progressively more assertive, even aggressive. By mid-May, for example, the executions were explained as the product of "the sad legacy of hate of the dominant class for the victims of its oppression." By October of that year the executions were being represented to its readership as "brutal deeds of murder," carried out in a "spirit of rancorous hatred" for the Irish race and people. With the implementation of

The Irish Canadian,

A WEEKLY NEWSPAPER

DEVOTED

TO THE INTERESTS OF THE IRISH PEOPLE.

Published every THURSDAY by the

TORONTO PRINTING COMPANY

LIMITED

At their Office, No. 40 Lombard Street.

SUBSCRIPTION, ONE DOLLAR PER ANNUM,
Payable in advance.
Two Dollars Per Annum if not paid in advance.
No Subscription taken for less than one year.

Advertising Rates made known at the Office

Letters and Correspondence should be addressed Canadian Office," Toronto, Ont.

PATRICK BOYLE,
Managing Director.

martial law and mounting support for an Irish republic, given clearest expression in the by-election victories of Sinn Fein in early 1917, the *Register* expressed its conviction that the Union, "forged for the enslavement of the Irish people," was a moral pariah. With the remarkable showing of Sinn Fein in the British general election of December 1918, and London's continued refusal to cede complete independence to Ireland, the *Register* insisted that the relationship of Ireland to England had become that of "Egyptian bondage."[69] The British empire itself stood not for progress and democracy, but the oppression of subject peoples. It had the following to say in May 1919.

> [T]he English had the world convinced that they themselves were the only chivalrous and noble race in the world, a race who would scorn to take an inch of extra territory, or to deny freedom to any small nations;--and just then these Irish reveal the skeleton in the closet and give the whole show away! And incontinently Egypt and India join in the row till the distracted world stops its ears and the hideous scandal of the British Empire family compact is bruited and bellowed abroad among the nations of the Earth![70125]

The greatest vitriol, however, was again reserved for Ireland's Protestants. When the British government announced--in light of the hostility of Ulster unionists to being included in an Irish state--that the only way forward was to partition the island, the *Register's* response was one of bitterness. Noting that the Ulstermen had resolved to "repudiate" not only Ireland but their own Irishness, and present 'Ulster' to the world as a nation unto itself, the *Register* denounced Ulster's Protestants in the harshest language. They were nothing but the "descendants of a pack of greedy and unscrupulous paupers and adventurers who crossed the narrow sea [and] settled like a swarm of carrion birds on the homes and lands from which the native Irish had been driven." They were nothing but "robbers and spoliators, and cannot repudiate a land which was never lawfully theirs." If they would only follow up their bold words "by quitting the island altogether, and ridding it of their hateful presence, what a blessing they would confer on the land!"[126]

Opinions were polarising. Protestant advocates of Irish Home Rule and Canada's Irish Catholics, in agreement on the Irish issue before the war, were now moving in starkly different directions. This trend was not only restricted to the Catholic press however. In January of 1919, for example, a mass gathering of Irishmen had been called for in Montreal. The meeting was announced with the issue of a circular declaring that the current condition of Ireland was deplorable, and describing the British premier, Lloyd George, as "a demagogue and a charlatan." It declared that "Self-Determination for the smaller nations gives Ireland an equal right with others to enjoy the long-delayed satisfaction of her national aspirations." "Freedom without stint and without measure," it continued, was "the only policy for England to employ." At the meeting itself, Charles Foy, president of the Canadian branch of the Ancient Order of Hibernians, described Sinn Fein as "the best and most logical movement that Ireland has ever had."[127] When the Self-Determination League got itself up and running in 1920 not a few Irish Catholic Canadians quickly made their way into its ranks.

But many of those Irish Canadians who did speak out in support of Sinn Fein, or who did join the Self-Determination League, must have slept uncomfortably at night. There was clearly an internal conflict of loyalties within such persons, and a certain degree of self-deception. For example, at a Toronto protest meeting, a Catholic priest, after thoroughly castigating British rule in Ireland, stated, oddly enough, that Sinn Fein "did not want separation but affiliation with Britain on terms of equality." Other meetings broke up with rousing renditions of 'God Save the King'. Canada's Catholics, after all, read the same secular dailies as did Protestants, and, as noted earlier, virtually every daily took the side of Great Britain. Some were critical of the British government over certain terms of procedure, but remained adamant that Irish grievances were largely unfounded (or self-inflicted), and that separatism was unthinkable. And from other pro-Home Rule journals Irish Catholics could expect no more. The Toronto *Globe*, for example, had the following to say on word that some fifty Canadians had travelled to meet with de Valera in Plattsburg, New York.

> Perhaps many Canadians of Irish birth or descent sympathise with Sinn Fein because they think it expresses the present mood of the majority in Ireland, but the *Globe* believes that few of them would be so unpatriotic as to join de Valera in his mischievous propaganda and plotting in the United States, which are reacting already upon Canada in the form of commercial threats. Irish-Canadians who are Canadians first should repudiate the noisy agitators who are misrepresenting them.[128]

From the countless politicians who had helped advance Home Rule in the pre-war era not a single initiative. Irish Catholics, a long way down the road to cultural assimilation, found themselves situated in a political culture that would not tolerate the activities of the Self-Determination League.

Powerful members of the Roman Catholic Church also spoke out in condemnation of Irish separatism. In December of 1920 the Bishop of Victoria, British Columbia, issued a pastoral loudly condemning those who might support the policies of Sinn Fein, stating that "self-determination as a full measure of Home Rule *within the Empire*, is what we stand for both as Catholics and Canadians." Responding to criticisms of his position published in the *Statesman* he wrote that it was not "compatible with our position as Canadians to help Ireland to cut herself adrift from the Empire." Nowhere, he stated, was the Roman church freer from persecution and political interference, or hindered "in carrying out her God-given mission than under the British flag"--a flag that, despite

Irish-American allegations to the contrary, stood mightily for democracy and freedom.[129]

IRISH CATHOLICS AND THE THIRD OPTION

One other factor, not unrelated to the foregoing, served to inhibit Irish republicanism in Canada, and that was the availability of the middle path of dominion status. If Ireland's Catholics would no longer accept Home Rule as a resolution of the question, and British self-interest would not permit a republic, then perhaps a form of independence within the empire might work. The remarkable thing about dominion status, after all, was its lack of definition. Canada was not a dependency, nor was it fully independent. Beyond that few agreed on Canada's constitutional position within the empire. Given the elasticity of dominion status, therefore, many Canadians--and certainly most Irish Canadians--believed that the Canadian precedent of 'Dominion Home Rule' was now the answer to Ireland's ills. This option was given great play on both sides of the Atlantic after May 1920 when a Canadian, Sir Hamar Greenwood, was sworn in as Great Britain's chief secretary for Ireland.[130]

From the beginning of the Home Rule debate in the 1880s, Canadians had been aware of the magnificent elasticity of 'the Canadian precedent'. It meant as many things to as many people who cared to utter the phrase. This had been both its strength and its weakness. The one thing it did not mean, however, was republican status, and few Canadian advocates of Irish 'separatism' actually envisioned, or desired, an independent Irish republic. This held as true for the Irish Catholic community in Canada as it did for considerable numbers within the Self-Determination League itself. Although the League's leadership officially pronounced it to be eternally hostile to any solution short of a republic, the rank and file membership thought differently. Several provincial branches of the League issued statements in support of dominion status, and expressed great disappointment in the irreconcilable position of de Valera. After the formation of the Irish Free State, the Edmonton branch met and decided to dissolve. In Winnipeg, the Canadian Irish Association--a cultural society--replaced the League. Toronto's *Catholic Register*, vehement in its earlier denunciations of Great Britain, offered its unconditional support. Most other Catholic papers were equally enthusiastic. The *Catholic Record*, for example, had the following to say in December of 1922.

> The Irish Free State is an accomplished fact. The action of the British Parliament in carrying out with scrupulous loyalty the provisions of the Anglo-Irish Treaty has given Ireland her place amongst the self-governing nations of the British Commonwealth--that great, happy group of sister-nations that have realised the ideal toward which the nations of the civilised world are yearning and slowly groping their confused way.[131]

--CHAPTER SEVEN--

> If there is an element in the British empire which is especially entitled to speak in favour of self-government, which is able to present examples taken from its own history of the benefits of self-government...I think the French element is especially entitled to do so.[132]

FRENCH CANADIANS AND IRELAND (1867-1925)

Although this book is largely concerned with the response of English-speaking Canada to the Irish Question, it remains absolutely necessary to take a look, however briefly, at the response of French-speaking Canada. This is important because French Canadians were an important source of moral support for Irish Canadians in their campaign on behalf of Home Rule. They were among the most consistent in their support of the Irish cause, and held a common disdain for the imagined forces of 'reaction' in Ireland and Canada alike, not least of which was the Orange Lodge. There was a common religious faith, a common minority status, and a common reluctance to accept unmitigated majority rule that bound the two communities together.

It will be noted, however, that the *limits* of French Canadian interest in the Irish Question were equally as real. In fact the key factor in translating sympathy for Irish nationalism into parliamentary resolutions was the partisan battle for the Irish ballot. This factor, it must be stated, also explains most of the parliamentary interest at the federal level. It is important, therefore, that before we discuss the extent of genuine sympathy offered to Irish nationalists by French Canadians, that the *political* be placed in the context of, well, politics! To do this I have relied on S.W. Horall's excellent Masters Thesis, *Canada and the Irish Question: A study of the Canadian Response to Irish Home Rule, 1882-1893.*

In this work the author establishes beyond a doubt the role of partisan politics in the introduction and prosecution of pro-Home Rule (and anti-coercion) resolutions in the Canadian House of Commons and provincial legislatures. Once this is established, the chapter will proceed to look, in greater detail, at other forms of French Canadian support for Irish nationalism. Here again, however, it will be seen that popular support for Irish separatism, even Irish republicanism, must be viewed within the context of French-English rivalries within Canada itself. In short, Irish nationalism was often grasped by French Canadians as a stick with which to batter Orange Ontario.

IRISH QUESTIONS AND IRISH BALLOTS

As mentioned earlier, many Irish Canadians were resolved to bring the weight of the Irish Catholic vote to bear on Canadian politicians. Opponents of Home Rule in Canada may have exaggerated the extent of opportunism behind the pro-Home Rule resolutions in parliament, but it cannot be denied that competition for the Irish ballot was a very important factor. It was no coincidence that the first resolution of 1882 was introduced by the Tories, the party with which most of the Irish in Canada were associated. Most Irish MPs sat on the Tory side of the House, and their support was recognised by the appointment of an Irish Catholic to the cabinet of Sir John A. MacDonald. And it was an Irishman, John Costigan, member for Victoria, New Brunswick, who initiated the first resolution in 1882. Costigan wrote to MacDonald in 1882 informing him that in response to "the expressed wishes of several influential Irish Citizens of the Dominion I intend at an early day, moving in the House of Commons for an address to Her Most Gracious Majesty the Queen in relation to the Irish Question," and requesting his support. The weight of the Irish vote was such that, although MacDonald and several members of both parties were strongly opposed to the notion, it nevertheless passed unanimously.[133]

MacDonald, opposed to the idea of meddling in the United Kingdom's domestic affairs, had advised

Costigan to drop the idea. Having failed in this endeavour, he reluctantly supported Costigan's initiative. He was, after all, well aware that if Costigan did not proceed with the Irish issue, Timothy Anglin, or some other prominent Irish Liberal would do so, and in a more assertive fashion. And the *Irish Canadian* was already on record for threatening retribution to anyone opposing the resolutions. "To those who may obstruct or defeat the resolutions we say beware! If the government is a party to such a crime, let us Irishmen everywhere in Canada rise as one man to strike them at the polls."[134] With a federal election only two months away it was a serious threat. Most members of parliament did not rely on the Catholic vote, but enough did to cause concern. A few seats, after all, could cost an entire election. By keeping the initiative within the party, moreover, he was able to persuade Costigan and the Irish caucus to tone down the rhetoric, making the resolution as unobtrusive as possible.[135]

In 1886, the date of the Home Rule bill's introduction into the British House of Commons, the electoral clout of Canada's Irish was again evident. This is evident in that, in 1886, MacDonald was most reluctant to partake in any new Home Rule resolutions. With the denial of self-government to the Metis, and a growing secessionist movement in Nova Scotia, Home Rule for Ireland had embarrassing implications for the Conservative government. MacDonald's increasing reliance upon the Orange ballot, moreover, was cause for concern, especially now that Orange Ulster was beckoning to them for moral and financial aid to *oppose* Home Rule. Costigan, therefore, was persuaded to settle for sending a personal telegram of support to Parnell reaffirming the support of the Irish members of the House of Commons for a measure of Irish devolution. The resolution of 1882 had, after all, been snubbed by the British government. Why risk further alienating the very British politicians on whose good will Ottawa depended for so much? The Irish Canadian, however, accused the Conservatives--and the Irish Tories in particular-

-of failing Ireland in its moment of need. It expressed the hope that when called upon, the leader of the Opposition, Mr. Blake, would not fail them also. And he did not. On the day following the announcement of Costigan's telegram to Parnell, Blake, to the Tories' dismay, rose in the House to move another resolution in support of Home Rule. When Blake's resolution was put to the vote, it passed unanimously. Despite strident opposition from individual members on both benches, not one felt capable of voting against it. The following year witnessed yet again the effect of the Irish vote, when the House of Commons passed resolutions against the British Conservative government's heavy handed policy of subduing the unrest that afflicted the Irish countryside after the failure of the Home Rule bill. While implementing many reforms, British Tories had resolved to defeat any attempts at insurrection with an iron fist--a policy which Irish Canadians bitterly resented.[136]

The year 1887, however, also witnessed the very real limitations of the Irish ballot. In Ontario, for example, the provincial election of 1883 had witnessed the flowering of a personal friendship between the Liberal leader, Oliver Mowat, and the Irish-born Roman Catholic Archbishop of Toronto. This resulted in the Archbishop agreeing to use his influence for the Liberal Party, and on election day most Irish voted for Mowat's Liberals, who went on to form the government. Another result of this was that the provincial Conservatives, under W.R. Meredith, decided to abandon the Catholic vote altogether and focus on wooing the province's ultra-Protestant Orange element. Although the anti-coercion resolution introduced by Mowat in 1887 passed handily, due to the Liberal's majority, not a single Tory sided with the government. Every one voted against the resolution. Having abandoned the Irish ballot, any compulsion to take up the Irish cause had disappeared.[137]

Another indication of the Irish community's limited influence came in the wake of the resolve of William O'Brien, a prominent Land Leaguer and nationalist member of the British parliament, to bring his battle to Canada. While Canadian legislatures were working on resolutions protesting coercion in Ireland, the Land League was actively opposing the eviction of tenants from the estates of none other than Lord Lansdowne, Canada's governor general. O'Brien had resolved that it would be a publicity coup for the cause if he shadowed the governor general across Canada. The trip, however, was a fiasco. It was one thing for politicians to woo the Irish vote, but for a suspected Fenian to come to Canada and assault the Queen's representative was another. At his meetings in Hamilton and Kingston he was shouted off the stage. At his Toronto rally a demonstration organised by Goldwin Smith and the mayor of Toronto ended in a near riot. And although many Irish members of parliament undoubtedly sympathised with his cause, not one was willing to meet with him. His very appearance in Canada was a setback for the Irish cause.[138]

Nothing did more to hurt the Irish cause prior to 1919, however, than the passage of time and the scandal leading to the fall of Parnell. With every passing year Irish Canadians became that bit less Irish, that bit more assimilated into the dominant culture. In Toronto, for example, the 1890s witnessed a sharp drop in both the number of branches of the Ancient Order of Hibernians and the number of adherents within each branch. It also witnessed the closing of the *Irish Canadian*, and the ascendancy of journals dedicated to the advancement of Catholic--as opposed to exclusively Irish Catholic--interests.[139] This 'de-greening' process was, of course, further advanced by the Parnell scandal, his denunciation by the Catholic Church, and the bitter divisions that followed his removal from the party leadership. Irish Catholics in Canada were deeply demoralised, and despite the Archbishop's prominent position on the stage at the Blake rally of September 1892, the days of Irish political clout in Canada were fast fading. When, in Blake's absence, an Irish MP rose in the House to introduce a new resolution of support for Irish Home Rule, it got absolutely nowhere. After a very brief debate the House took a recess after which it proceeded to other issues. As far as

Canadian politics was concerned, Ireland, at least for the moment, was no longer a profitable cause.[140]

By 1903, however, the Irish community had recovered from the demoralisation of the 1890s and elements within that community were again pressuring for another resolution of support from the House of Commons. The British government had just introduced the latest in a long series of land reform packages. Irish nationalists at home and abroad, however, feared that this latest initiative, and its massive allocation of funds to redress Irish grievances, might just succeed in derailing Home Rule. It had to be met by a renewed effort in support of the Irish Party, and in the Canadian parliament a resolution in support of Home Rule was again passed. But here again the limits of the Irish ballot were again apparent, as the federal Tories, having aligned themselves with Ontario's ultra-Protestant element, voted almost unanimously against the measure.[141] When that party attained power in the election of 1911 noone even bothered suggesting a resolution of support for Irish Home Rule. The Irish ballot had no weight with that government.

THE IRISH QUESTION IN QUEBEC

The pattern governing the parliamentary resolutions was identical in Quebec City. As in Ottawa the resolutions of 1886 and 1887 were initiated by Irish Catholic members of parliament. In 1886 the initiative was taken by Felix Carbray, an Irish Catholic member for Quebec West.[142] In 1887 it was initiated by another Irish member, Mr. Owen Murphy. The tone and language of the resolutions was again similar to those moved in Ottawa. The 1886 resolution read in part as follows.

> Be it Resolved, that this House, always
> sensible to everything tending to the
> greater welfare, progress and happiness
> of every nation of the Empire, desires
> to award its warm appreciation and
> great pleasure on the initiation in the

> Imperial Parliament, of legislation of
> a character to give a local government
> to Ireland.[143]

The following year, after protesting the introduction of coercive measures in Ireland, the legislature again called for the granting of an Irish parliament at Dublin. That the initiatives-- not to mention the wording of the resolutions-- originated from Irish members is clear. Few French Canadians ever expressed such concern for other nations of the empire, or revelled in pan-imperial sentiment. That was the world of English Canadian thought, and, to a lesser extent, Irish Canadian thought. That Quebec politicians were as pragmatic as their English Canadian counterparts is a certainty. And it is little surprise that, in the wake of the Irish community's disarray after 1887, no new resolutions were entered into parliament at any level. There was no pressure to do so. Once the threat of Irish retribution at the ballot box passed, so did the Home Rule initiatives in the country's legislatures. No new initiative was introduced in the Quebec legislature, and when Charles Devlin introduced his resolution in the House of Commons no French Canadian threw his support behind his measure.

It is not to say that there were no politicians who genuinely favoured Home Rule for Ireland-- there certainly were--but, as elsewhere, without Irish backing the matter would certainly never have been introduced into the Quebec legislature. Quebecers, after all, were North Americans. The affairs of France were of little interest to them. Why issue such concern over Ireland? Quebecers, it should be remembered, were constantly striving to convince English Canadians that their emotional home should be firmly set in North America, and that it was time to let go of Britannia's apron strings. If Canada was to work it was imperative that English Canada direct its vision inward. It would not do to have their bodies in one place and their hearts elsewhere. This may have been an unfair evaluation of English-Canadian imperialism, but it was how many francophones thought. It is unlikely, therefore, that such persons would have shown the level of interest in Ireland's affairs as the legislative resolutions suggested.

There was also the deterring factor that Canada's Irish Catholics, despite their common faith with the Quebec majority, were viewed as anglophones. And for considerable numbers of Quebecers the French language was the key to their identity in North America. Their Catholicism was shared with numerous ethnic groups, but the French language was theirs. And few were unaware that Canada's Irish, outside the province of Quebec, had proven themselves to be less-than-enthusiastic advocates of French language rights. When push came to shove over language, Irish Catholics quickly fell into line with the rest of English-speaking Canada. Simply put, the common cause implied by Quebec support for Irish Home Rule was as much myth as reality. Nevertheless, for those who did embrace the Irish cause that affinity was strong. For others, advocating Ireland's national rights served well as a stick with which to beat English Canada.

For some of those French Canadians who were genuine in their support for Irish nationalism, the failure of the Canadian Irish to rally behind French language rights in Canada was more than offset by Ireland's devotion to the Catholic faith. Henri Bourassa, one of the most enthusiastic French-Canadian advocates of the Irish cause, had the following advice for his compatriots.

> To those of you, my brothers in language, who occasionally speak harshly of your Irish compatriots, allow me to say that however powerful are the local quarrels, the entire Catholic Church owes to Ireland and the Irish race a debt which every Catholic has a duty to pay. For three centuries Ireland has, under violent persecution and in the face of the most insidious attempts in a time of peace, given us such an example of perseverance in morale and faith in demanding its

> rights that all Catholic people must envy it instead of reproaching it.[144]

But what motivated many other French-Canadian advocates of Irish Home Rule, and invigorated those who genuinely admired the faith of the Irish, were the many parallels that appeared to exist between the Quebec and Irish situations. First of all, the most vocal challenger of Ireland's national aspirations was none other than the Loyal Orange Lodge, the same body that regularly obstructed the proliferation of French language rights in Canada. An ultra-Protestant body it had also been at the forefront of anti-Catholic agitation across Canada, not least in Quebec. At least French Canadians had their provincial autonomy to fall back upon to defend their cultural and confessional interests when besieged by Orangeism. The Irish didn't even have their language! Large numbers of Irish, moreover, had been thrown into the midst of Protestant Ontario to face the same organisation that had obstructed their national ambitions at home. And Quebecers were aware that nowhere did Orangeism flourish outside the province of Ulster as in the province of Ontario. As early as 1844 six out of ten city aldermen belonged to an Orange Lodge, and in the following year the city elected its first Orange mayor. Between that year and century's end all but three of Toronto's twenty-three mayors belonged to a lodge.[145] More often than not, the city treasurer, deputy treasurer, solicitor, and commissioner were also Orangemen. The post office, the customs house at the federal level, and the police and fire departments, waterworks, and gasworks at the corporate level were likewise Orange reserves. Such was the influence of the Order in Ontario's capital city, notes Gregory Kealey, that politicians "built or demolished their careers in proportion to lodge support."[146] And although the Orange Order quickly took on a Canadian tone and character after its arrival in Toronto in the early 1800s, it never successfully distanced itself from its Irish origins. One of the social highlights of the calendar year, for example, was the 'Glorious Twelfth' when Orangemen walked to commemorate the victory of William III and Irish Protestantism at the Boyne. Colourful marchers, and banners depicting both an Irish and a Canadian heritage, and common struggles against Rome, lined the streets of the city. It was inevitable, therefore, that a certain amount of respect and empathy would have gone out to the Irish community. It is also inevitable that, despite their linguistic quarrels, a certain common cause bound the two communities together.

This sense of empathy with the Irish would also have been reinforced by an awareness that both groups had been conquered by the same opponent. In 1759, of course, French rule in North America ended with the British victory on the Plains of Abraham. For French Canadians the conquest was the central fact of their history. Ramsay Cook noted the following in one of his numerous books on French-Canadian nationalism.

> [T]he history of French Canada since 1759 has been the story of the gradual, but unceasing, movement of French Canada towards a political status which would finally erase the stigma of the Conquest. That is the central event in French-Canadian history, and the one that each successive generation of French Canadians attempts to come to terms with. Conquest implies subordination and inferiority. The cure to conquest, to subordination and inferiority, is equality. But what is the meaning of equality?[147]

There were, simply speaking, two basic versions of equality in French Canadian thought: those who believed the consolidation of provincial rights was the best method of defending French rights, and those who preferred to actively engage the federal government in that end.

The confederation settlement had, of course, given to Quebec, the province where the vast majority of French Canadians lived, a government of its own. It was a provincial government within a highly-centralised political system, but it had allowed Quebec City control over those areas deemed essential to the survival of the French fact in Canada--education, religion and civil law. By being part of Canada, however, French Canadians could share in the potential wealth of an expanding nation. From 1867 on, however, this dualism would exist uneasily. The acceptance of Canada as 'theirs' depended on English Canada's acceptance that confederation was a compact not merely between provinces, but between peoples: the British and French. This understanding would dictate that the French and English languages, and the cultures that cradled those languages, be deemed equal from Atlantic to Pacific. Canada had to be as much theirs as English Canada's. The same held for the federal government. When English and French interests collided the interests of the French minority in Canada must be protected. By aligning itself with other vested interests at Ottawa many French Canadians believed that their weight could be sufficient to determine this.

Others were less optimistic, convinced that it was a foregone conclusion that Canada would be dominated by Anglo-Saxon Protestants, and that, in times of crisis or conflicts of interests, French Canada would be the loser. The way forward for Quebec was to jealously defend, and then build upon, the established provincial rights given Quebec in 1867. Such persons believed their convictions to have been confirmed by the trial and execution of Louis Riel in 1885--a fact that convinced many that French Canadians could not expect to be treated as equals outside of their own stronghold. The schools crises, where the provincial governments of Ontario and Manitoba moved to reverse the privileges of French language instruction in their provinces, also served to alienate Quebecers.

There was also the matter of Anglo-Protestant domination of foreign policy matters to alienate French Canadians. Simply put, French Canadians disagreed fundamentally with their English-speaking counterparts over the correct relationship of Canada to Great Britain and the empire. For countless English Canadians imperialism was a positive good, and none were more convinced of this than the advocates of imperial federation. The Imperial Federation League had been founded in Great Britain in 1884, with its first Canadian branch opening in Montreal the following year. For its Canadian advocates imperial federation was a way for Canada to progress beyond colonial status without separating from the empire, or falling into the arms of the United States. Led by George Parkin, Colonel Denison and George Grant it combined a form of Christian mission and anti-Americanism. Its main focus was to promote the notion that the dominions should participate in the making and executing of imperial foreign policy. To this end it advocated the setting up of an 'imperial legislature' in London with representatives from Britain and the overseas dominions. Although many English Canadians were uncomfortable with the notion of transferring any powers from Ottawa to London, throughout the period under examination most continued to express their nationalism within an imperial context. Nationalism and internationalism, or imperialism, were complementary, not inimical, to one another. Even in the minds of those Anglo-Canadians who possessed a deep distrust of English politicians--and they certainly existed--nationalism often meant little more than securing a greater voice for Canada in the empire's corridors of power.[148]

Many English Canadians, moreover, preferred to think of their empire as Anglo-Saxon and Protestant. George Grant, for example, had the following to say on the matter in 1890.

> The Empire to which we belong is admittedly the greatest the world has ever seen.... It is world-wide and therefore offers most opportunities for all kinds of noblest service to humanity, through the serving of fellow-citizens in every quarter of the globe. Let Canada ask for some emblem--let it be maple leaf or beaver--to represent it on the flag that represents so marvellous a past and present. Is it to be thought that we would separate from

> such a flag without cause, still less
> place our country in a position of
> antagonism to it? Think what it has
> always represented--personal and national
> freedom; civil and commercial,
> intellectual and religious freedom...and
> the proclamation of eternal life to
> every son of Adam.[149]

Clearly French Canadian Catholics were not going to embrace the empire in this fashion. Simply put, there were two key approaches to United Kingdom-Canada relations embraced by French Canadians. The first school revolved around Henri Bourassa. At a time when most English Canadians were stressing the British nature of Canada he was adamantly opposed to having Canada's fortunes tied in any way to those of Great Britain. Since the British empire was an Anglo-Saxon entity it could not be embraced by French Canadians. It was inconceivable that English Canadians could not see this. That English Canadians did fail to see this, therefore, only retarded Canadian nationhood, and postponed the day of national reconciliation. Besides, the natural evolution of societies was toward national sovereignty. Only independence would convince English Canadians that Canada was their true home. Canada must pursue its own interests therefore, not those of Great Britain. Canada should only go to war if attacked. As to the merits of British colonisation of the globe, Bourassa had only contempt. He denied to any nation, "however grand it may be, however high its aspirations, however noble its traditions, however numerous its fleets, however powerful its armies, the right to impose its yoke, beneficial or harmful, on other peoples of the earth."[150] This applied as much to Ireland as to India or Egypt.

The second approach to imperial relations is associated with Sir Wilfrid Laurier, Canada's first French-Canadian and Roman Catholic prime minister. Unlike Bourassa, Laurier tended to see the British empire as an agent of progress and liberty in the world. He certainly did not embrace the notion of its Christian mission, but saw it as a secular force for good. Canadian nationalism, moreover, was fully compatible with membership within a decentralised empire--so long as it *was* decentralised. He adamantly opposed any concession of Canadian autonomy to imperial federation schemes and used the Imperial Conferences to further the cause of voluntarism. It was in Canada's interests to be part of the British empire, but the nature of the link with Great Britain should remain undefined--a moral and voluntary union as opposed to a legal compact. He did believe, however, that the imperial sentiments of English Canadians must be respected, and that, in foreign policy, be accommodated within reason. Canada, he insisted, was founded upon compromise and it was no time to stop now. To this end he attempted to secure compromise on the main issues of contention during his premiership of 1896-1911, including the Boer War and Canadian contributions to the Royal Navy. Whereas Bourassa insisted that Canadians should stand aloof from British imperial ventures, Laurier insisted that compromise was possible.

Laurier was equally insistent that Irish nationalists put aside their more fanciful notions and work for a settlement that respected the interests of Ireland and Britain alike. If the people of England were satisfied that Ireland's Roman Catholics would remain loyal under Home Rule, he had insisted during the debate on the 1903 resolution, "I am sure the next day home rule will be granted to Ireland." But, he acknowledged, not every Briton believed this, and Irishmen were as responsible for this distrust as anyone. He said to Mr. Costigan on this matter...

> I must say to my hon. friend, the mover of this resolution--that some of the Irish leaders have acted very unwisely and have unfortunately given cause of distrust against them. If I had the privilege of a seat in the House of Commons, I would say to my friends the home rulers: While I sympathise with you, while I am, as much as you are, in favour of home rule for Ireland, I want it to be understood, and I want to say

> here and now, that home rule does not
> mean separation; you should and you
> must be loyal to the Crown.

As an advocate of a decentralised empire, but aware of Britain's legitimate security needs and the sensibilities of the Irish minority, he insisted that compromise was essential. If British anxieties could be addressed then Home Rule was a certainty. A fair and equitable settlement of the Irish problem, he insisted, was immensely desirable, being "a blessing not only to Ireland but to Great Britain, to Canada, to Australia, and to all parts of the British empire in which Irishmen are to be found."[151]

FRENCH CANADA AND THE SELF-DETERMINATION LEAGUE

Despite Laurier's moderation, nothing did more to increase French Canadian sympathy for Irish self-determination than the Great War and the nature of Canadian involvement in that conflict. When the First World War broke out in August of 1914 there were two diametrically-opposed opinions as to what Canada's role in the war should be. For English Canadians it was inconceivable that Canada would stand aloof. Any threat to the empire threatened Canada. For most French Canadians, however, the European conflict was just that--a European conflict being fought between a number of vested interests, none of which affected Canada. It was a case of one imperial power challenging the influence of another over a given area of real estate. There was nothing noble about Britain's role in the conflict. London was motivated as much by self-interest as was Berlin, Moscow or Paris. In no conceivable way did the war threaten the welfare of Canada, and Ottawa should tell Great Britain that it had no intention of taking sides. Should Canadian soil be threatened Canadians should rally to its defence, but not a moment sooner.

For his part, Robert Borden, the Conservative prime minister of the day, had promised Quebecers that although Canada would certainly go to Britain's aid, the Army would be manned exclusively by volunteers. No French Canadian would be coerced into fighting a war to which they were opposed. But as the war progressed and Canadians at the front endured great losses the pressure to impose conscription mounted in Canada. Conscription received a further impetus from the international prestige Canada was attaining by its triumphs in the field. Many English Canadians were basking in the fact that their country was a contender in the conflict in Europe. There was also a growing conviction among many in English Canada that, contrary to the assertions of Quebecers, great moral principles were at stake in Europe. This was not a conflict of like imperialisms. Whereas Great Britain stood for fair play and democracy, Germany championed autocracy, militarism, and brute force. Other tyrants were watching to see if the kaiser could get away with his European venture. It was imperative that he be stopped. For many in English Canada, therefore, the war had become a crusade of sorts. That French Canadians stood aloof from it was the source of considerable bitterness. In 1917, therefore, the Borden government went to the electorate to ask its permission to break the promise of 'no conscription'. The country divided largely along ethnic and religious lines during the election. Fiery rhetoric from both sides of the debate served to alienate and embitter relations, and when the Anglo-majority granted the government leave of its obligation to Quebecers the response in French Canada was one of anger. For many it reinforced once again that Quebecers were second-class citizens in their own country. Riots spread across the province and resistance to conscription efforts were mounted on a large scale. By the time the war concluded, French and English Canadians were divided as never before.

These developments had served to reinforce the sympathy of many Quebecers for the perceived plight of the Irish. But here again the battle being fought was deemed by most French Canadians to be a Canadian battle, with shillelaghs the weapon of convenience, not of choice. In his 1906 work *The Race Question in Canada* Andre Siegfried captured well the depth of racial and religious animosity in Canada. He noted that, as a conquered race, the French had suffered more than was commonly supposed from the attitude of their conquerors. For all the euphemisms employed in official language, "the English treat them too often as inferiors and aliens, whose slightest progress they look at askance as menacing the security of the State." He correctly observed, however, that, in the French psyche, "the conqueror is not England herself, distant and invisible, but the English Canadian who lives on the spot and profits in his insolent way by the victory of his ancestors." The British government actually enjoyed a certain prestige as a distant, supreme arbiter to whom appeal of grievances was not always made in vain.

> [T]here is no feeling of hatred towards England; on the other hand, there is no feeling of affection. When English armies are defeated upon the battlefield, as in the Transvaal War, the French Canadians experience no extravagant grief. They even rejoice quite openly, but that is to rile their Ontario neighbours and to enjoy the diversion of treading a little on the lion's tail; it is a taste of revenge in which they indulge their injured *amour propre*.[152]

This was certainly a major determinant in French Canadian sympathy for the Irish cause after the Great War. But their common experiences during the war had only cemented that sympathy. Both had fought bitterly against attempts to have conscription imposed upon them during the war, and both had been subjected to the abuse of those who demanded that they give their lives in another's war. When the Self-Determination League for Ireland was founded in 1920 many French Canadians were in full agreement with its analysis of the Irish conflict and the ill effects of imperial sentiments in Canada. In November of 1920, at a national convention of the League being held in Montreal, the chief speaker was none other than

Henri Bourassa himself, speaking on the Irish and Canadian questions for close to three hours. The Quebec provincial branch of the League, moreover, had two French Canadians serving as vice-presidents: Lucien Cannon and Armand Lavergne. The latter was particularly bitter in his denunciation of British policy in Ireland. Addressing a League meeting in Montreal he had denounced England as "the greatest murderer of small nations," dwelt at length on British crimes in Ireland, and declared that, as a Christian, he could justify Sinn Fein rebellion so long as the Union Jack gave shelter to murderers. Irish Canadians and visiting Irishmen were clearly anxious to develop on this sense of common purpose. One prominent Irish guest at a Montreal meeting, after justifying Sinn Fein, hoped that "henceforth French-Canadians and Canadian-Irish would fight together for faith and liberty."[153]

The Self-Determination League clearly attempted to capitalize on this potential alliance by castigating Anglo domination of Canada, and the restrictions on French language rights outside of Quebec. Nor was it wary about digging into the ancient past to find evidence of British oppression in Canada. In April of 1920, for example, the *Statesman* stated the following.

> Our school law makes obligatory the hoisting over every public school, of the Union Jack of Britannia who rules the waves.... The flag of an Empire that is at this moment maintaining a diabolical tyranny in Ireland...The flag that flew at the masthead of the warships that England sent to perpetrate the foulest dead in the history of the New World; the dispersion of the Acadians.[154]

But even here there were limits to French Canadian support for the Irish cause. If the truth were known most French Canadians couldn't have cared less about Ireland, and those who did--Bourassa included--were hardly resolute republicans. Quebec, after all, was a very conservative, ultramontane society where revolutionism and republicanism brought back dreadful memories of the violent anti-clericalism of the French Revolution. Most of the province's politicians, at both the federal and provincial levels, were committed parliamentarians and genuinely admired British political institutions. Bourassa himself was raised to admire the British parliamentary system, and had often described himself as a Liberal "of the British school."[155] It is unlikely, therefore, that even he shared the more bitter anti-British sentiments of the Self-Determination League. But for the time being, given the deep divisions created in Canada by the war, support for the League served as a convenient emotional outlet for many French Canadians.

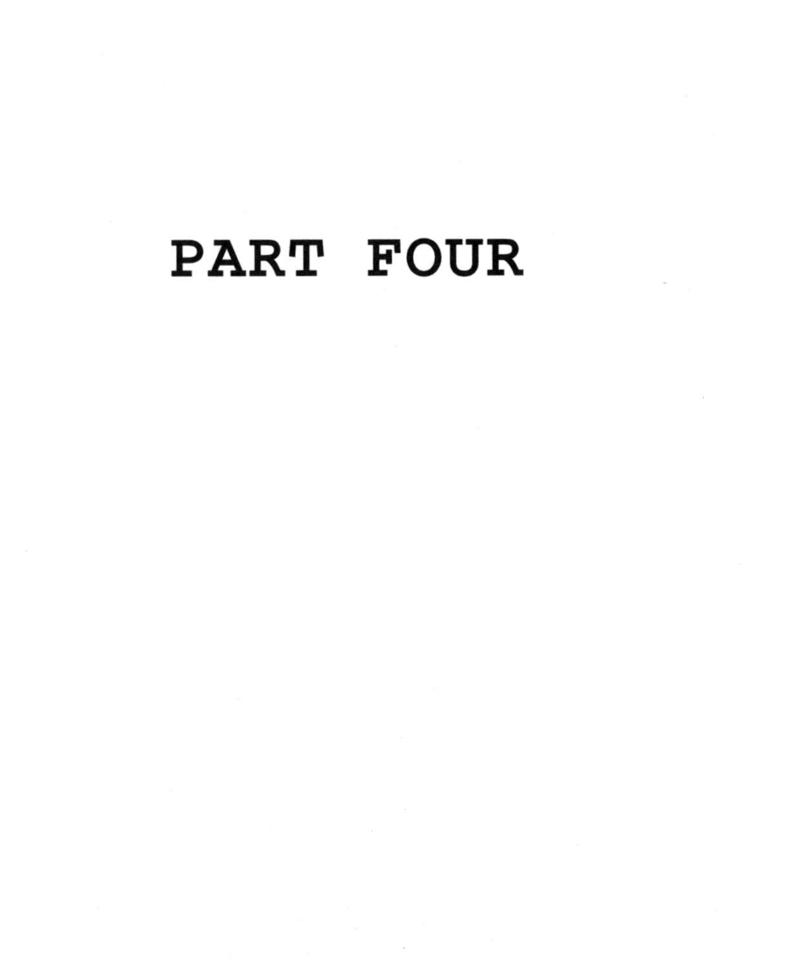

PART FOUR

--CHAPTER EIGHT--

FROM FREE STATE TO REPUBLIC (1925-49)

In the years spanning 1925 and the proclamation of the Irish Republic in 1949, opinion in English Canada went through three distinct phases. The first, oddly enough, was defined by a sense of benign indifference mixed with an optimism that Irish nationalism was done with 'extremism'. Relationships at the inter-dominion level also seemed to be putting to rest the greater fears of those who had opposed Irish independence. Despite constitutional and political developments in Ireland that bore no resemblance to those of Canada, there was a certain momentum that found the Free State and Canadian governments temporarily share common cause. For some it appeared a stroke of good fate that, for most of the 1920s and 1930s, Mackenzie King was the Canadian premier. King, while expressing a genuine affection for the crown and commonwealth, believed that the ties that bound should be as loose as possible. Whereas Robert Borden had viewed Canada as a British country that ought to play an active role in the development of the British empire, to Mackenzie King Canada was a North American nation that ought to disengage from international affairs. He repeatedly asserted that the empire/commonwealth should be a voluntary association of equals--a cultural and moral partnership moreso than a political union. King, after all, was the successor to Sir Wilfrid Laurier, a man who greatly admired British institutions and saw countless benefits in being associated with the British empire, but who had repeatedly emphasised the voluntarism of the commonwealth link. King was also the grandson of the famous Scots-Canadian rebel, William Lyon Mackenzie. Leader of the 1837 Upper Canada rebellion aimed at securing greater democratic freedoms for the colony's people, he had gone down in Canadian history as a great reformer. As prime minister, therefore, Mackenzie King could converse comfortably with his Irish counterpart. One could distrust English politicians and yet embrace the empire. Increasingly, moreover, the various components of the empire could embrace it on their own terms.

There is even some evidence that King intentionally kept the bogey of Irish separatism before the British government as a warning not to block further constitutional progress. On at least two occasions Ottawa warned the British government, as well as his own critics in the Canadian parliament and press, that unless Dublin was allowed to make further constitutional progress, it would leave the empire. In this manner Mackenzie King, the ultimate pragmatist, also used the Irish predicament to further his own political agenda. The old question of 'How can Canada be of service in furthering the happiness of Ireland?' had always been modified, or even driven, by self-interest on the part of Canadian politicians. 'How might Irish intransigence better serve the Liberal Party's desire for a greater measure of Canadian autonomy?' was now the new appendage. In Ottawa and Dublin alike there were significant forces dedicated to loosening the ties that bound. And if such decentralising forces helped reconcile Ireland to continued membership in the commonwealth, all the better.

Equally important was the absence of a lobby in Canada between 1922 and 1939 for a more doctrinaire approach to Irish affairs. Not only had post-war Irish unrest disillusioned many Canadians who had previously advocated the Irish cause, there was a soft consensus on the matter of increased autonomy within the empire. When, in 1922, Great Britain had asked Ottawa to send a contingent to support London in its conflict with Turkey over the Chanak peninsula, Ottawa immediately declined. And, unlike the South African conflict two decades earlier, there was little internal pressure for it to consider otherwise. Where in God's name was Chanak, Canadians asked themselves. Noone knew, and relatively few cared. The 1920s were a decade in which countless Canadians sought an escape from the demands and disappointments of idealism in hedonistic excess. If the Irish wished to waste their time and their lives re-fighting hopeless battles, so be it. Canadians weren't interested. After four hard years of war Canadians simply wanted to enjoy the material things of life, and for most of the 1920s these things were in abundance. Besides, Ireland appeared to be coming to its senses. The *Canadian Annual Review* noted the following.

> In 1925 the Irish seemed to be turning away from politics and constitutional issues toward constructive measures. In seven By-elections in the Free State it became clear that the tide was against the Republicans as the enemies of settled peace. The Government spokesman put forward a progressive platform including agricultural development, electrical development, housing, tax reduction, relief of unemployment. They appealed for support as the builders against the wreckers. Polling took place on March 11, the Government winning all seven seats.[156]

Even the boundary question appeared to have disappeared from the Irish political landscape. Two years later the *Canadian Annual Review* was still able to say that the period under survey was "in the main one of progress in the Irish Free State."[157] In January of the following year, Cosgrave, the Irish premier, visited Canada and was well received.[158]

In the 1930s Canadians were distracted from Irish affairs, and foreign affairs generally, by the Great Depression. Bread and butter issues were of greater interest to most Canadians than abstract notions of sovereignty or *independence*. This preoccupation with bread and butter issues was also prominent in the Canadian media commentary that there was. On word of de Valera's election victory in 1932, for example, the *Ottawa Journal*, sensing trouble, suggested that it was in Ireland's interest that he shelve his nationalist aspirations and, as his predecessors had done, address the material needs of his people. "What Ireland needs," it argued, "and her needs approximate to most countries--are better living conditions, fewer slums in places like Dublin, more of education for her people, more of decent shelter and clothing and of the amenities of life for her population." These things, "not senseless strife over whether Ireland should be a two-by-four republic, will give Irishmen the chance they deserve to have." The whole world had placed "entirely too much stress upon an often meaningless political freedom. People are only free in a measure that they are economically free, financially independent, possessed of certain things in life which make for self-respect and self-reliance."[159]

Some commentators were adamant that time and economic reality would do just that. The *Victoria Daily Times*, for example, stated that although de Valera was still his irreconcilable self, "a term in control of affairs at Dublin very probably will mellow him as office has mellowed other firebrands."[160] Others were more optimistic yet. "The people of Ireland," stated the *Montreal Daily Star*, "have shown themselves more than capable of Home Rule and of successfully guiding their own affairs."

> They have just passed through an election in which forces which have been bitterly criticised have come uppermost--and noone has the slightest uneasiness...Chronic critics of democracy were staggered when Labour came into power in Great Britain; but today, in the greatest crisis that country has faced since the war, a Labour leader is Prime Minister and many of his Labour colleagues are co-operating with the spokesmen of other parties to so resolutely govern the nation that Mr. Baldwin today announces a balanced budget this spring.[161]

Even de Valera's decision to exploit the occasion of Edward VIII's abdication in 1936 to abolish the post of governor general and the oath of allegiance was seen as the move of a newly moderated politician. "President de Valera," noted the *Victoria Daily Times*, "does not seem to know what he wants." Not so long ago, it noted, "he had seemed ready to move heaven and earth to establish a republic, independent entirely of Britain and the rest of the Empire." That he did not seize the occasion of Edward's abdication to declare a republic was as noteworthy as his decision to abolish the Oath and post of governor general. The reason for de Valera's newly-found timidity could be found in the political and economic realities that now confronted him. "The stage play of the last day or so...is not a very convincing reaffirmation of his original desire." Rather, it suggested that, having learned a few things while in office, "the old attractions of defiant separation have lost a good deal of their glamour."

THE SECOND WORLD WAR: 1939-45

If a cautious optimism dominated English-Canadian attitudes to Ireland between 1923 and 1939, this was certainly not the case between 1939 and 1945. These were, after all, years of unprecedented ideological and military confrontation in Europe and the Far East, and while Canada, Australia, South Africa, New Zealand, and Newfoundland threw their resources into the war effort, Eire, alone among the dominions, chose to remain neutral. And this neutrality meant allowing Nazi Germany to maintain an embassy in Dublin while denying Britain access to the strategically-significant naval ports on Eire's coast. When the war first began many Canadians expressed disappointment that Ireland, the country whose cause so many Canadians had advocated on the assertion that Irish separatism would not jeopardise British security one iota, had opted for neutrality. Some held that surely saner minds would soon prevail. Surely once Ireland had made its point that Irish foreign policy was henceforth to be made by Irishmen, it would come to the aid of the empire and to the defence of democracy. After all, had not Mackenzie King waited a full week before throwing Canada into the fray to emphasise a similar point? Many believed that all would be well in time. But when Eire remained resolute in its determination to maintain its neutrality, even through the darkest days of 1940-41, Canadian disapproval often turned to bitter resentment. Like Churchill himself, many were genuinely convinced that Ireland's position on the war was morally indefensible, and in stark contrast to the principles of freedom for which Dublin claimed Irish nationalism had always stood. Others emphasised the illegality of Eire's neutrality when the crown itself was in jeopardy.

Most critics, however, reproached Eire from a conviction that Irish neutrality, and de Valera's refusal to allow British ships into Irish ports, was responsible for the heavy losses inflicted on British and Canadian shipping in the north Atlantic. From the Irish bases, it was asserted, escorts could have sailed further out into the Atlantic, providing the necessary cover for hard-pressed convoys. Destroyers and corvettes could have refuelled quickly, and tugs sent to rescue ships in distress. From these bases, the Battle of the Atlantic would have been fought on equal terms. As it was, the bases were denied. Escorts had to go the 'long way around' to get to their destination, and return to harbour at least two days earlier than would have been necessary. The cost in men and ships, although difficult to calculate, was certainly substantial. One particularly vocal member of parliament, reminiscent of those who opposed Home Rule in an earlier era, had the following to say.

> In the firm struggle in which Britain is now engaged only one thing can deprive her of victory. If her sea communications with the arsenal of democracy across the Atlantic are cut, the war for her is lost. Ireland lies across those lines of communications. An Ireland fighting on her side would make those communications safe, while a neutral Ireland would imperil and has so far gravely imperilled them. With Ireland in the possession of her

enemies, the vital arteries would be severed.

Many Canadians also disapproved of Eire's stance from a conviction that the war being fought was no less Ireland's war than Britain's, or Canada's.[162] Others were clearly annoyed that, while many Canadians had consistently offered their support for Ireland's right to self-government, Ireland now appeared indifferent to the reality of Canadian sons perishing in the cold Atlantic. Criticism also emerged from a popular belief that this war was different from any other in modern memory. Great moral and political principles were at stake. To an extent rarely occasioned in history, the present conflict was clearly one of right versus wrong. That Nazi Germany might be permitted to win the war was unthinkable. In such a conflict, to sit aside while the war raged was to abrogate one's responsibility as a democrat, and one's responsibility as a Christian. To remain neutral when the war turned decisively in favour of Germany was unconscienable.[163]

These same sentiments rang throughout the daily press. "It does not matter to de Valera whether the British Empire is wiped out tomorrow," concluded the *Montreal Daily Star*. "Indeed, he might welcome it."[164] The *Toronto Globe* added that, given Eire's intransigence, it was "the natural and inevitable thing for Britain to occupy those ports of the country best fitted to resist attack." History would not look kindly on a government that failed to deal quickly with "this menace at England's very door."[165] Eire's determination to allow Germany to maintain an embassy in Dublin during D-Day preparations in mid-1944 also brought bitter denunciation, as did de Valera's decision to send a letter of condolence to the German consulate upon news of Hitler's death. "Not even Franco, who practically lived in Hitler's breast pocket," complained the *Vancouver Sun*, "has descended to that depth."[166]

Some commentators, it is true, were willing to be more understanding of de Valera's position. An article in *Macleans* magazine in January 1942, for example, had argued that most of the charges against Eire were ill founded. Accusations that Eire was abuzz with German agents, and that the government looked aside while the IRA collaborated with Berlin, were "a fantastic absurdity." The German Minister in Dublin had five employees; he could not communicate intelligence matters to Berlin without their communications passing through Allied channels; and he could not have agents throughout Ireland since Eire had no German population whatsoever. As for the IRA, 800 of its members were in internment camps. Eire's firemen fought Belfast's bomb fires, and countless thousands of Irishmen were fighting in the British forces. To ask anything more of Eire was unreasonable. Eire, it argued, hadn't one modern anti-aircraft gun in the entire country. It had no tanks, anti-tank guns, mechanised divisions, heavy artillery, or Air Force. In such circumstances Eire's entry into the war would be suicidal, leading to wholesale massacre of totally unprotected citizens. It might even spark an IRA uprising, creating division and confusion that Hitler would quickly move to exploit.[167] On a less pragmatic note another commentator, speaking before the Empire Club in February 1940, insisted that it was also in the interest of democracy that Eire be left to its ways. After all, was it not democracy for which Britain and its allies had gone to war? What better example of democracy in action could there be than allowing de Valera to keep his country out of the war. When the war is won and history is written it will go down as another example of Britain's greatness and confidence in its mission in the world.[168]

It appears that Mackenzie King himself shared such an opinion. While anxious that Eire should enter the war on the Allies' side, King was fully aware of de Valera's reasons for not doing so. After all, Canada's own recent past had witnessed severe rioting in Quebec when Ottawa had introduced conscription during the First World War. And even now King was forever wary of a potential insurrection in Quebec should Ottawa be required to introduce conscription a second time. Most importantly perhaps, King was a politician who joyed in taking pragmatism to new heights. He believed a negotiated solution was desirable because both the United Kingdom and Eire had legitimate concerns. Britain needed access to the ports, and de Valera had serious reasons for not granting them. All the time Germany was sitting back rather pleased with the dilemma. A negotiated settlement, not an imposed solution, was the answer, and this he communicated to the Allies on several occasions.

As 1943 gave way to 1944, however, de Valera's stated case against participation in the war continued to be taken apart in the English-Canadian press. Most believed that dramatic changes in the prospects of the Allied nations had served to dismantle de Valera's case against participation in the war. The virtual destruction of the Luftwaffe, for example, had removed the possibility that Berlin might respond with a bombing offensive against Irish targets. As American and Canadian troops began arriving in southern England--and, for that matter, Northern Ireland--in preparation for the D-Day operations, de Valera's case against fighting in 'Britain's war' also rang hollow. There was also the great moral imperative of protecting the lives of the vast numbers of southern Irishmen serving in the British Army and Royal Air Force. An exasperated *Montreal Daily Star* pointed out the following in March of 1944.

> Naturally, nobody expects Mr. de Valera ever to take any action…[which could] be conceived as friendly to the British, but in this particular instance if he fails to act as requested he is in reality placing the lives of scores of thousands of fine Irish soldiers in jeopardy....These men are fighting for the preservation of world freedom. If Mr. de Valera persists in retaining in Eire agents of Germany and Japan who are known to have been engaged in supplying information inimical to Allied interests, he is therefore deliberately risking the lives of many thousands of his fellow-

citizens whose sense of justice and right transcends their political hatred.[169]

The arrival of the Americans and Canadians also added dramatically to the number of persons of Irish extraction amassing in southern England. It seemed inconceivable, therefore, that de Valera could be so blind to his obligations as a Christian and an Irishman. "The position of Eire as a State," added the *Halifax Herald*, "has never been creditable in this war, but today, on the eve of vast operations in the West, it is less creditable than ever."[170]

Even Mackenzie King had his limits. When, on the eve of D-Day operations, the American government had issued a tersely worded diplomatic note to the Irish government, protesting the continued presence of Axis embassies in Dublin, de Valera appealed to Canada and Australia to intervene in Washington to have it withdrawn. King refused, informing the Irish ambassador that he fully shared in the sentiments expressed in the note.

THE REPUBLIC OF IRELAND

In 1949, only a few years after the war's conclusion, Eire proclaimed itself a republic and left the commonwealth. For many in Ireland this was seen as a natural step in Ireland's path to sovereign nationhood. In Canada, however, there were some who were not willing to let the proclamation of a republic pass without bitter comment. This was perhaps inevitable given Dublin's decision to have the republic come into effect on 24 April 1949--the 33rd anniversary of the 1916 Easter Rebellion. As the *Globe and Mail* noted disapprovingly, "the 1916 rebels expected German help and a German victory in the war. The military fortunes of the British nations and their Allies were then at a low ebb and the prospect of their defeat was indeed a source of inspiration for the rebels."[171] It appeared to many to be a calculated insult to those critical of Eire's role in the war, and as an insult it was taken, at least by some.

Others, however, simply saw it as evidence of political immaturity, and as yet another reason for Canadians to detach themselves from Irish affairs. Many Canadians expressed a sense of bafflement regarding Dublin's long-term objective. Could the Irish government not comprehend that, by proclaiming a republic, it had permanently alienated the one segment of Ireland's population it ought to be wooing? When the Ulster elections of February 1949 returned a considerable unionist majority at Stormont the *Globe and Mail* put it down to the imminent proclamation of a republic.[172] It seemed uncanny that, given India's resolve to reconcile its republican status with commonwealth membership, that Irishmen could not be more creative. While some commentaries expressed a sense of bafflement, or, more commonly, exasperation, others yet expressed a profound disinterest. They commented on the independence day ceremony only because it marked the closing point in a drama in which Canada and Canadians had once been key players. For most of the previous century Canadians had been active on both sides of the Irish debate, offering various propositions that might help alleviate Irish grievances while reconciling Ireland to the British empire. There was considerable disagreement on how to accomplish that, but everyone was in accord that Ireland, however governed, should remain within the empire. When Cosgrave announced that a republic was imminent, it appeared to mark the end of Canada's stake in Ireland's political fortunes. Those Canadians who had advocated a form of Home Rule or dominion status had believed that they were offering a *via media*, a reasonable compromise between contesting interests. In the end Ireland opted to follow the American model, and there seemed little reason for Canadians to offer further guidance.

--CHAPTER NINE--

THE NORTHERN IRELAND CONFLICT (1969-)

By the time the latest round of Irish troubles began in 1969 the world was a very different place from what it had been in 1949. In sharp contrast to the Home Rule era, the Canadian experience was rarely held up as a credible way forward for Northern Ireland. There were minor exceptions of course. Republicans had toyed with the idea of a federal Ireland as a solution in the 1970s, while loyalists had thought aloud about the possibility of an independent Ulster dominion based on the precedent of Canada, Australia and New Zealand. This latter notion, temporarily embraced by prominent members of the paramilitary Ulster Defence Association, would have severed the constitutional link with the British government while maintaining the link to the crown. A workable compromise some thought. Around the same time the British government was thinking aloud about the best means of securing compromise in Northern Ireland. Under the heading "Government Could Draw on Canadian Experience in Announcing New Initiatives for Ulster", the *London Times* revealed the following.

> The Government is expected to announce its new initiatives for Northern Ireland this week. It is understood the Canadian federal experience has been considered as a possible pattern for meeting minority rights and claims in Ulster.

But as the article stated, such analogies were basically useless. If Canadian constitutional garments were to be cut down to fit Ulster everything depended on whether it was the Catholic minority which was seen as requiring 'Quebec status' within Northern Ireland (or the United Kingdom), or whether Protestant Ulster was seen as requiring Quebec status within a united but federal Ireland.[173]

In the end no political initiatives based on the Canadian experience ever got off the ground, not least because they were highly unrealistic. The Canadian government, absorbed with an internal ethnic conflict of its own, also showed no interest in involving itself in the Ulster Question. In the end the extent of Canadian involvement in Northern Ireland, at least prior to the IRA cease-fire in 1994, was financial, with the Shorts aerospace industry being the best example of Canadian financial input. This detached approach to the Irish conflict on the part of the Canadian government was also motivated by the fact that, like the world around it, Canada had changed. Cultural, constitutional and demographic changes had ensured that the Irish conflict was now only of passing interest to most Canadians. There was virtually no political pressure for Canadian politicians to get involved, and they did not. This chapter, after introducing the reader to the key political developments in Northern Ireland between 1969 and 1994, will address the theme of Canadian cultural transformation at greater length.

CIVIL RIGHTS AND CIVIL WAR

Since partition Northern Ireland had been governed by one political party to the exclusion of all others, the Ulster Unionist Party. In open elections it had been returned time and again by the Protestant majority in electoral contests which focused on one issue: the Union with Great Britain, for or against. In the first-past-the-post system that Northern Ireland shared with the rest of the United Kingdom it was inevitable that such an outcome would emerge. The problem, however, was that in a deeply divided society such as Northern Ireland the excluded minority, in this case the Catholic community, inevitably remains alienated from the system of government. Catholic grievances were further aggravated by electoral gerrymandering on the municipal level which ensured Protestant majorities on city councils representing Catholic-majority districts. Catholics also nursed economic grievances against the Northern Ireland state. On average, Catholics had a higher unemployment level, lower incomes among those employed, and restricted access to new housing.

In their own defence, unionists reminded their critics that Ulster's Catholics also enjoyed the benefits of the British welfare state not available to their co-religionists south of the border. They also lived in a country where violence, political or otherwise, was a rarity. A murder was something to be talked about for months. They also pointed out that Catholic schools were generously funded, that unemployment also plagued the Protestant community, and that Catholics were just as likely as Protestants to discriminate in favour of their own. The only difference was that Protestants held the reigns of power and, as in most divided societies, used this asset to benefit their own. After all, had Catholics not consistently shown themselves to be disloyal to the state? Had they not, in their blind pursuit of a united Ireland, steadfastly refused to co-operate in the building of an Ulster in which they might feel more at home? Had they, and their representatives, not undertaken one initiative after another to undermine the state of Northern Ireland? If Catholics had disabilities under the Northern Ireland regime they were, unionists argued, largely self-inflicted.

Nor, they argued, was the Republic of Ireland without blame. The 1937 constitution had laid claim to all of Ireland in a move unprecedented in all of Europe. Many countries, unionists pointed out, hold irredentist ambitions, but the Irish Republic was unique in having that ambition entrenched in its constitution. If Ulster's Catholics were unwilling to cooperate in the building of Northern Ireland it was in no small part due to the Republic's relentless insistence that the Northern Ireland state was an illegitimate entity. When Dublin sought overseas support for this position, unionists were deeply resentful of the Irish Republic, and of what Belfast considered its 'fifth column' within Ulster itself--the Catholic minority.

Regardless of where the blame should be laid for Catholic disadvantages in Northern Ireland, it cannot be denied that Catholic grievances were deeply felt. After all, had the north of Ireland not been their ancestral home long before the first Protestant set foot on the Antrim coast? Being second-class citizens in one's own land is a bitter pill to swallow, regardless of where one is located on the globe. But for Ireland's Catholics there was hope yet. If African Americans could force major concessions out of the great American republic, Ulster's Catholics could surely rock what Bernadette Devlin liked to describe as the 'tuppence-happeny' state of Northern Ireland. In 1967, therefore, the Northern Ireland Civil Rights Association was founded to advance the interests of the Catholic minority on the streets of Northern Ireland. Between that time and August 1969 the NICRA held mass rallies across Northern Ireland, demanding several key reforms. For their part, Protestants led counter-demonstrations, convinced as they were that the NICRA was merely a front for the IRA. Catholics hadn't even the decency to conceal that organisation's name from the new body's title! To Protestants, therefore, the NICRA had nothing to do with civil rights. It was the same old republican ogre in new clothing, in yet another effort to fool world opinion. Catholics were, after all, determined to destroy the state of Northern Ireland. Why would they wish to see it reformed?

The government of Northern Ireland, however, was willing to acknowledge the legitimacy of many of the Catholic community's grievances. Captain Terence O'Neill had reached out to the Catholic community in recent years by making some significant gestures of reconciliation. In 1965 he had invited the prime minister of the Republic of Ireland to Stormont for talks on how the two Ireland's could better work together as neighbours. Sharing a small island ensured that, despite political differences, there existed many areas where co-operation would be of mutual benefit. O'Neill, however, had a significant number within his party who were unhappy with such gestures. The followers of the Rev. Ian Paisley were especially adamant that O'Neill's coddling of Dublin was nothing short of treason. O'Neill had to go. As for Ulster's Catholics, their hopes of important reforms had been raised only to be dashed. The violent Protestant response to their street protests only further served to embitter inherited grievances and convince many Catholics that both unionism and Northern Ireland were irreformable. When the annual loyalist Apprentice Boys parade passed by the Catholic working class enclave of the Bogside in August 1969 the violence that ensued led to a complete breakdown of law and order. Such was the state of anarchy that on 13 August British troops were dispatched onto the streets of Northern Ireland to maintain law and order. While initially resented by unionists and welcomed by Catholics (as greatly preferable to the 'B Specials' and Royal Ulster Constabulary) the dynamics of the situation quickly changed. The IRA immediately took advantage of the presence of British troops on Irish soil to raise the old irredentist cry of 'Brits Out'. If guerrilla tactics could spur the British into repressive measures to restore order in the North, then the long-awaited revolution was on.

In early 1970 the IRA began a major bombing and assassination campaign, and the security forces responded as the IRA had hoped. On August 4th of the following year the Northern Ireland government introduced internment without trial for suspected terrorist suspects. It was the biggest tactical blunder the security forces could have made. Doors were kicked in at four in the morning, men dragged from their beds in front of their wives and children, sons thrown into armoured vehicles and taken away indefinitely. The fact that only Catholics were initially interned, and that the Army was incredibly slow in releasing information about the whereabouts of internees, indicated to Catholics that the British Army had taken sides. The IRA had been handed its ace card. While there had undoubtedly been a certain amount of abuse dished out at the hands of the Army, Sinn Fein, the IRA's political machine, now turned out endless tales of torture in British 'concentration camps'. If internment was intended to suppress violence, it clearly had the opposite effect. Violence soared as young Catholics flocked into the IRA to carry on the ancient struggle against the British state. If their brethren in the south could toss the Brits out so could they. While the IRA bombed and sniped, Catholics demonstrated against the Special Powers Act in increasing numbers. Despite a government ban on marches by either side, one such demonstration had been planned for Londonderry on January 30th 1972. What ensued was a crowd that turned on the Army, and an Army that responded by shooting dead 14 protesters. While the security forces insisted they were fired on first and simply returned fire, Catholics adamantly denied the charge and accused the Army of cold-blooded murder. Bloody Sunday was born and the image of British soldiers standing over dead Catholics became etched into the nationalist consciousness.

BRITISH POLITICAL INITIATIVES

In the aftermath of Derry the British government soon became convinced of the need to secure tighter control of military operations in Ulster. They were also increasingly aware of the Catholic community's permanent alienation from the existing political arrangement in Northern Ireland. In March of 1972, therefore, London suspended the Northern Ireland parliament for a period of one year and called on unionists and constitutional nationalists to be imaginative in defining a new political settlement. The only precondition demanded by London was that any settlement have broad cross-community support. The settlement arrived at, the Sunningdale Agreement, kept Northern Ireland British while guaranteeing to Ulster Catholics a certain percentage of cabinet seats in any new government. Alongside power-sharing there was also to be a Council of Ireland consisting of elected members of the Northern Ireland Assembly and the Irish Dail. While Protestants were divided on the merits of power sharing, most were vehemently opposed to the concept of a Council of Ireland. It was nothing less than a republican Trojan horse constructed to lull Ulster unionists into a united Ireland. Could it be that London was now in cahoots with Dublin in nudging Ulster out of the United Kingdom? It wasn't impossible in the minds of many. After all, had not the British government tried to coerce Ulster out of the UK in 1912-14 by threat of arms? The Agreement was unacceptable, and in the February 1974 British General Election the anti-Sunningdale unionists took a majority of the votes in Northern Ireland, and 11 of the 12 Northern Ireland seats at Westminster. Meanwhile, opposition was mounting on the streets, and on May 24, the day the package was to be ratified by the new Assembly, a province-wide strike was called by the Ulster Workers Council. Two weeks later the unionist members of the executive resigned, bringing the Assembly to an end, and a return to direct rule. Britain's first political initiative was a resounding failure.

London's second major attempt to secure an internal solution came one year later when the government announced elections to a Constitutional Convention to see what provision for the government of Northern Ireland was likely to command the most widespread acceptance throughout the community. In its earliest stages the convention would simply serve as a forum for discussion among Ulster's constitutional parties, and then allow matters to progress on their own time. It failed to even get off the ground. The Alliance Party (the major non-denominational, small 'u' unionist party) proclaimed the merits of power-sharing while the Ulster Unionist Council (an alliance of the major unionist parties) demanded a return to majority rule. As for the Social Democratic and Labour Party (SDLP), the main constitutional nationalist party, it refused to even contemplate any scheme that offered anything less than a Council of Ireland and power-sharing, and fought the election on an abstentionist platform. The Convention lasted five months.

London's third political initiative, 'rolling devolution', was undertaken in 1982 in the wake of the bitter divisions aroused by the IRA hunger strikes. Having replaced Humphrey Atkins as

Northern Ireland secretary in 1981, James Prior quickly announced that he would stake his political reputation on returning political stability to Northern Ireland. He argued that unemployment, and lack of confidence in the future, was at the core of unrest in Northern Ireland, and that the uncertainty surrounding direct rule inspired little hope of attracting desperately needed foreign investment. And little progress against the paramilitaries could be made until jobs could be found for Ulster's youth. Again, the Assembly's task would be a modest one at the outset. Its responsibilities would be to 'debate and report', and to 'monitor and scrutinise' the work of the various government departments where they affected Northern Ireland. And once there was 'sufficient cross-community support' power would once again be devolved to Stormont on a departmental basis. In time even responsibility for security matters might be returned to the province. The unionist parties fought the elections and took their seats while proclaiming their unmovable opposition to power sharing or a role for Dublin. For its part the SDLP again fought the election on an abstentionist platform. No power-sharing, no Irish dimension, no deal. And without the SDLP the necessary 'cross-community support' was unachievable. The unionists continued to exercise their scrutinising powers, however, until the assembly was dismissed by the new secretary of state, Tom King, in 1986.

The fourth, and most significant, political initiative undertaken by the British government was that of the Anglo-Irish Accord of 1985. The Accord was the result of long negotiations and discussions undertaken by Margaret Thatcher and Charles Haughey in 1980 in an attempt to surmount their substantial disagreements over Northern Ireland. An Anglo-Irish Intergovernmental Council was set up to oversee the discussions, discussions which progressively became more agreeable after the election of Garret Fitzgerald in 1982. The Accord resulted in a mutual conviction that both traditions deserved to be safeguarded in Ulster; that the aspirations of both communities were equally legitimate; and that combined efforts were required to defeat terrorism. While breaking from past precedent of securing significant cross-community support for any political initiative, and pushing unionist concerns aside, the Accord did recognise Northern Ireland's position within the United Kingdom. Article 1, Sections a and b stated the following:

The two governments

> (a) affirm that any change in the status of Northern Ireland would only come about with the consent of a majority of the people of Northern Ireland;

> (b) recognise that the present wish of a majority of the people of Northern Ireland is for no change in the status of Northern Ireland;[174]

The Accord further declared that if, at any time in the future, a majority of the people of Northern Ireland formally consented to the establishment of a united Ireland, both governments would introduce and support in their respective parliaments legislation giving effect to that wish.

Significantly, however, the United Kingdom government also accepted that the Irish government could put forward views and proposals on matters relating to Northern Ireland. There was to be no area of administration where Dublin could not have the ear of the British secretary of state. In fact, at the time of signing, proposals were already being considered regarding the re-routing of Orange parades, the removal of the Ulster Defence Regiment (UDR) from Catholic neighbourhoods, and the creation of new institutions to reflect the identity of the minority community. In effect, the SDLP had been granted its Irish dimension, and Dublin had won a voice in governing Northern Ireland without the violence and social upheaval that unification would inevitably cause. In return, the loyalists received Dublin's assurance that it acknowledged

Ulster's present constitutional status, as well as its promise to redouble its efforts against IRA operators in the Republic. As for the British state, it had won a diplomatic coup. With the stroke of a pen, England's Irish problem had also become Ireland's Irish problem.

Cracks in the wall appeared immediately, however, as unionists rallied against the Accord in vast numbers. On the Saturday following the Accord's signing, 203,000 loyalists demonstrated outside Belfast City Hall. For them, the Accord was yet another step in the gradual process of pushing Ulster out of the United Kingdom and into the Irish Republic. Their suspicions and fears were heightened by the fact that while Dublin was in almost daily contact with the SDLP, not once were unionist politicians consulted by London regarding their concerns and interests. In fact, Mrs. Thatcher had repeatedly assured the loyalist community that consultations were unnecessary since no deal was even being contemplated. When the truth became known the unionists associated the government's 'secrecy' with 'duplicity'. Unionists also wanted to know why the wording of the Accord was left so ambiguous as to allow for two dissimilar interpretations of its implications in the two parliaments; why the Accord was not presented to parliament for debate before ratification; why Northern Ireland's 'present status' was not defined; and why the Agreement presented to the Irish parliament and that to the British parliament had different titles. Such were the concerns that even the Alliance Party, although it reluctantly supported the deal, appeared to be splitting along denominational lines. On the day of the November demonstration the 13 unionist MPs at Westminster resigned their seats and called a bi-election as a referendum on the issue. All 13 anti-Agreement candidates were returned to their seats with significant majorities.

On the other side of the divide, the IRA rejected the Accord as unworthy of discussion. If anything, they argued, it served to reinforce partition and legitimise the British occupation of the North. Dublin had betrayed its obligation to advance the cause of Irish unity, and the only resort left open to republicans was to redouble their struggle against the British state. Between the Accord's signing in November 1985 and the IRA cease-fire of 1994, over 700 people would lose their lives in political violence, and a considerably larger number would suffer serious injury. Political differences would mount between successive governments in London and Dublin as violence continued year after year with little sign of stopping. Whereas Dublin insisted that political co-operation should be emphasised, London continued to insist that cross-border security was at the heart of the Agreement. Despite high hopes in London and Dublin, not to mention Catholic areas of Northern Ireland, the Accord appeared to be another failure.

CANADA AND THE TROUBLES

Any discussion of Canadian responses to the Northern Ireland conflict must begin by emphasising that Canada was a very different country from what it had been as late as 1949. This was true on a number of levels. In terms of its constitutional relationship to the United Kingdom it was a fully independent member of the Commonwealth of Nations. As for the empire to which an earlier generation of imperialists had been so devoted, that entity was now gone. Whether one measured it in terms of trade, cultural affiliation, or attitudes, Canada's relationship with the United States was now of greater importance than relations with Britain. Its membership in NATO, the United Nations, and NORAD, moreover, all served to further weaken the British link. Two years previous, Canadians had elected as their prime minister Pierre Elliot Trudeau, a nationalist in his relationship with the United States and Great Britain alike. By the time Trudeau left office in 1984 he had repatriated the Canadian constitution from London, changed the name of the British North America Act to the 'Canada Act', and announced that Dominion Day would henceforth be called 'Canada Day'.

The decline of Canada's British Isles character has also been advanced by the radical restructuring of Canadian demographics. As late as 1945 Toronto was one of the most British and Protestant cities on the globe. The Orange Order still ran the show. Since that time Toronto's population has been radically transformed. By any measurement it is now one the world's most ethnically diverse cities. Three thousand kilometres away in Vancouver the same transformation has taken place. Once considered the backdoor to Europe, Vancouver now considers itself the front door to Asia. Other cities have also experienced demographic revolutions. Hamilton, Ontario, once a British city that recruited its police force through the local Orange Lodge, is now home to, among others, significant Italian, Portuguese, and Polish communities. While rural Canada largely remains Anglo-Protestant, the vast majority of Canadians now live in cities--cities that have welcomed wave after wave of newcomers since the Second World War. For many years now, Canada, in terms of population ratio, has accepted more new citizens than any other industrialised country in the world. Most of these new Canadians derive from Asia and Eastern Europe, not the British Isles.

Another trend affecting Canadian attitudes to Northern Ireland since 1969 has been the rapid secularisation of Canadian society. While most claim to be Christian, and profess a belief in 'God', relatively few attend church. Many teenagers have no clue as to whether they are Catholic or Protestant. They don't care. Prayer is no longer permitted in public schools and the Sabbath is another shopping day. For most of the past three decades every Canadian prime minister, with minor exceptions, has been a Roman Catholic-- and nobody has noticed. It has not been an issue because they have not allowed their religious tradition to affect their politics. The same can be said of former Ontario premier Bob Rae, who completed his four year term of office with most residents of Ontario unaware that he was Jewish. On the other hand, when Reform leader Preston Manning, an evangelical Christian, brought his religious baggage with him to Ottawa he became a lightning rod for abuse. Have your religion, be blessed by your religion, even preach your religion from the rooftops--just keep it out of politics.

It is this secular outlook that makes it extremely difficult for modern-day Canadians to empathise with either side in the Northern Ireland conflict. After a series of brutal events perpetrated by both sides in Belfast and Derry in early 1972, Canadian editorial commentary made this apparent. "The sheer insanity of what is now happening in Ireland," argued the *Globe and Mail*, "is something that even those most anxious to apologise for either side cannot accept, without placing themselves beyond the border of madness."[175]

Another sign of this detachment was the high number of newspaper editorials evincing ignorance of the entire situation in Ireland. Unlike in previous decades, Canadian newsmen and the Canadian public alike had to *relearn* the Irish Question. With the growing realisation that the Ulster situation was highly complex, out came the history books and the thinking caps. When the complexity of the conflict became evident the media coverage over the many years of conflict was generally respectable and balanced. What was missing from previous decades, however, was a passionate advocacy of either side's position. No grand solution was ever embraced as the answer to the Irish Question, as Home Rule had once been. Nor was any one particular option bitterly denounced. In fact, the more unreasonable nationalists and unionists appeared to behave the more distanced and analytical the media became. The *Globe and Mail*, for example, issued the following commentary when 13 Catholic protesters were shot dead by British troops in Londonderry in January of 1972.

> On any reading of the conflicting evidence, it seems possible that British troops were too quick to fire on the crowd of Irish Catholic demonstrators. Yet the crowd was at

least stoning those men, whose comrades have been steadily gunned down by Irish Republican Army snipers. Moreover the demonstration had been legally banned, for manifestly justified security reasons. The IRA command asserts that its men did not fire first. So they were there, then, and they did fire on the security forces. The claim that they only returned the troops fire, unlikely as it is, is thus immaterial. Clearly this was no ordinary civil rights demonstration: the terrorists were there for the deadly purpose of making sure that it was not.

"BUT, MONSIEUR, WHAT CAN I POSSIBLY TEACH YOU? YOU'VE BEEN IN THE BUSINESS MUCH LONGER THAN I HAVE."

Chambers, *Nanaimo Free Press*, 7 March 1972.

But the report wished to point out why Catholics were demonstrating and rioting in the first place. That it was all manipulated by the IRA was simplistic, and ignored the legitimate grievances of Northern Ireland's Catholics.

> Yet for all that it was illegal and dangerous, Sunday's Londonderry march began as an impressive demonstration of deep feeling in the Irish Catholic population of Northern Ireland. It was intended by its organisers and the vast majority of its 15,000 participants to be a peaceful protest against the draconian policies of arbitrary internment, the methods of interrogation used by the British forces and Ulster police in their war with the IRA, and the lack of any progress toward social and political justice in the province.[176]

Over the next 25 years the Canadian media would attempt to give balanced and informed coverage of the Irish situation. This was more true of the printed media than the televised media (which sometimes engaged in sensational reporting which served to confuse rather than inform), but, with a number of such exceptions, the latter also did a respectable job. Both, however, were unanimous in their condemnation of political violence. Whatever grievances the nationalist community had, they could be resolved without bombs and bullets. As for loyalist retaliation, it was also remarkably brutal, and, in the end, self-defeating. If Britain's will to remain in Ulster was to be sapped, it would be because loyalists began contributing to the IRA's plan to make Ulster ungovernable.

Despite the extensive coverage of the Ulster situation by the Canadian media, its commentary on Ulster's political options revolved around three key events. The fall of Stormont in 1972, the Sunningdale experiment of 1973-74, and the Anglo-Irish Accord of 1985. The more modest initiatives in between provoked little debate. The most extensively debated initiative of all was the decision to abolish Stormont in March of 1972. While the rare editorial in limited-circulation newspapers called for a united Ireland in the aftermath of Bloody Sunday, and others demanded that Stormont be left in place, most concluded that direct rule was the way forward. The *Globe and Mail* insisted that it was imperative that the British government take swift and effective action to prevent further deterioration of the situation. The most effective measure available was direct rule. This alone would allow for the necessary breathing space requisite to clear and rational debate.

As already stated, in its conviction that direct rule was the best way forward for Ulster, the *Globe and Mail* was accompanied by perhaps a clear majority of dailies. But well researched and thoughtful editorials did not necessarily dictate that every editorial reached the same conclusion. An editorial in the *Vancouver Province*, for example, came to a diametrically different conclusion from that of the *Globe*. On the matter of the suspension of Stormont it concluded that the British government had betrayed the loyal majority, given in to terrorism, and strengthened the Republic's irredentist claims on the North. The *Province* stated the following.

> Despite Mr. Heath's assurance the campaign against terrorism will be kept up, the suspension of the powers of a democratically elected government will be seen by the IRA and by world opinion as a victory for the gun. If it gives the terrorists renewed hope that their methods may eventually drive the war-weary British to abandon Northern Ireland altogether, the chances of peace will recede even further...Prime Minister Jack Lynch of the Irish Republic has predictably welcomed the Heath move.[177]

Others saw things very differently, and argued that direct rule, while a positive step in itself, must merely be a temporary stop on the road to a united Ireland. While no newspaper, to my knowledge, ever attempted to justify IRA violence, some asserted that such violence was symptomatic of Ireland's colonial legacy. As the complexity of the situation became clear, however, and Canadians came to appreciate the determination of unionists to resist incorporation into the Republic, the 'united Ireland' option was cast aside. But most agreed that, in such a bitterly divided society, majority rule was also untenable. A consensus quickly emerged that direct rule was the lesser of all evils, and should remain in place until Ulster's Protestants and Catholics learned to live together.

On the whole, therefore, the Canadian media was 'unionist' in its conviction that the border could not be removed until a majority in Northern Ireland consented to it. But it was not the unionism of the post-war years, when Ulster's retention within the empire was deemed of some concern to Canadians. With the passing of the empire, the Irish Question was increasingly viewed by Canadians as just that--an Irish question, of little or no concern to themselves. It was a more pragmatic approach to the matter that took root in Canada after 1969. By that year Northern Ireland had been an established fact for 50 years, and had enjoyed relatively stable government within a relatively democratic framework. To consider abolishing it against the wishes of the majority, as the IRA demanded, was unthinkable.

For Great Britain to depart from Ulster under the present circumstances, moreover, would certainly result in outright civil war. And most papers were content to portray the British government and British Army as honest brokers, eager to abandon Ulster to its fate, but restrained by a noble sense of duty. At times laudatory articles from the British media were reprinted in the Canadian press without further commentary.[178] Certainly individual members of the security forces were responsible for acts of violence against Catholics, and Mrs. Thatcher could be unnecessarily obdurate, but the overall consensus in Canada was that the British had made the best of a bad situation. Who would wish to be in their shoes? As for the Anglo-Irish Accord of November 1985, its authors were praised for their willingness to compromise in the interests of peace. In a country such as Canada, where, outside Quebec, nationalism was normally a low-key affair--a pastime as opposed to a burning obsession--the dogmatism of the competing nationalisms in Ulster seemed unreal. The Anglo-Irish Accord then, although imperfect, was a major step in the right direction. On the day after the Accord was signed the *Globe and Mail* described it as "a laudable and overdue attempt to wrest the initiative in Ulster from sectarian extremists." In doing so, moreover, they had laid siege to the nationalistic dogmas for which both sides had proved themselves willing to kill. It stated the following.

> Both Britain's Margaret Thatcher and Ireland's Dr. Garret Fitzgerald have chipped away at their respective sacred icons in return for concessions that may improve present conditions. Mrs Thatcher, despite the Accord's reaffirmation of British sovereignty over Ulster, has acquiesced in an informal dilution of that sacred trust in the form of the proposed Anglo-Irish conference...Dr. Fitzgerald's iconoclasm came in the accord's affirmation that reunification of the island will only be effected with the consent of Ulster's majority. This commitment may seem to be no more than realism...but it is the most explicit disavowal of Republican irredentism ever offered.

Despite certain omissions in the Accord, such as any mention of an extradition initiative on the part of Dublin, or the removal of the Republic's constitutional claim to Northern Ireland, the Accord was a remarkable achievement. In view of several failed attempts at securing an internal settlement agreeable to both communities, the consensus in Canada was that the Accord's weaknesses paled next to its boldness and originality.[179]

It is a certainty that the Accord's apparent reasonableness accounted for the decision of Brian

Mulroney (himself no champion of orthodox notions of sovereignty) to break convention and openly endorse the Ulster initiative. Mulroney, moreover, was himself of Catholic Irish descent, and fondly thought of himself as the embodiment of Canada's constitutional and Irish heritages alike--terribly reasonable and terribly accommodating! He had also come to power with an enthusiastic 'can do' approach to the Quebec situation. In 1982 the Canadian constitution had been repatriated by the Trudeau government over the objections of Quebec's separatist government, which was unhappy about some of the new provisions in the constitution, and simply refused to sign it. Ottawa's resolve to march ahead with repatriation only served to embitter French-English relations in Canada. Once in office it was Mulroney's resolve to reopen the constitutional issue by offering 'distinct society' status to Quebec, a form of compromise between the two competing versions of Quebec's rightful place in North America. The Quebec problem was solvable. All that was required was good will, strong leadership, and the ability to secure reasonable compromise. When the Irish government began contacting foreign governments in its bid to build up support for the 1985 Anglo-Irish Accord, therefore, Mulroney gave it his immediate and public support. After this initial endorsement, however, the Canadian government returned to its 'hands off' approach to the Irish question. Perhaps the significant difficulties encountered by Mulroney in his efforts to secure a new consensus on the Canadian constitution played a part. After all, as was the case in Northern Ireland, the deal was condemned by nationalists as inadequate, and by their opponents as another example of reckless appeasement. That the Anglo-Irish Council had failed miserably in its efforts to reduce sectarian violence in Ulster undoubtedly brought home to Mulroney the complexity of the Ulster situation. Failure inevitable. Don't make the effort.

Despite Mulroney's very brief interest in the Northern Ireland conflict, successive Canadian governments have been painfully aware of Canada's own ethnic divisions when analysing the Irish situation. If Mulroney's 'can do' approach to Quebec had compelled him to support the Anglo-Irish Accord, the Quebec situation had encouraged others to leave the Ulster situation alone. After all, in October 1970 the Trudeau government had sent Canadian troops into the streets of Montreal, suspended *hapaes corpus*, and implemented the War Measures Act permitting internment without trial. Almost five hundred persons were interned, of which only a small number were actually involved in insurrectionary activity. The government had been provoked into this highly controversial, and, many would say, unjustifiable, measure by the sporadic activities of the *Front de Liberation du Quebec* (FLQ), a terrorist organisation dedicated to Quebec independence. The FLQ had blown up monuments dedicated to British monarchs and war heroes, planted several explosive devices in post boxes, bombed the Montreal stock exchange, and kidnapped a British trade commissioner and a Quebec cabinet minister. The British commissioner was eventually released in return for the kidnappers' transport to Cuba, but the Quebec minister was executed for treason to the Quebec state.

Moreover, this new wave of Quebec nationalism had two main catalysts, at least one of which undoubtedly served to further deter Canadian intervention. One was the rapid decline of the religious aspect of Quebec's identity and the search for a replacement. The other was an ill-conceived endorsement of Quebec separatism by Charles de Gaulle while on a state visit to Canada in 1966. Addressing a large crowd of admirers from a Montreal balcony he had given his ringing endorsement of *'Vive le Quebec libre'*. With the exception of Quebec separatists, who were thrilled by such a dramatic endorsement of their cause by a French president, it was viewed by Canadians as an astonishingly inappropriate violation of protocol. He even had the gall to compare his enthusiastic reception along the route to Montreal with his entrance into liberated Paris in 1944. Had not Canadian graves helped make his entrance into Paris possible? Such was the outrage that the Canadian prime minister of the day announced that de Gaulle had outstayed his welcome and should immediately leave the country. The two didn't even meet.

These events further contributed to Ottawa's resolve not to get involved in the Irish situation, despite Dublin's expressed wish that it would. The request had come from the president of the Irish Republic during a visit to Canada shortly after the bloodshed in Derry in January 1972. The Canadian government immediately turned down the invitation, a move universally approved of by the press. It wasn't Canada's place to meddle. The *Calgary Herald* reported on the 'odd request' as follows.

> The Canadian government acted correctly in refusing to take sides in the Irish dispute...Canada would have put itself on the side of the Irish republic, scarcely a disinterested party in the Northern Ireland situation...He must have realised that Canada couldn't possibly do what Dublin asked. Canada has its own potential partition problem. It also has large numbers of citizens of Irish descent whose sympathies could be pointlessly aroused by any show of partiality on Ottawa's part. In any case, meddlesome outsiders would be likely to exacerbate the situation by intruding on the tense emotional state existing in Ulster.[180]

No, Canada should keep out of the Irish situation altogether.

Besides Mulroney's endorsement of the Anglo-Irish Accord in 1985, the only other case of political interest being expressed in the Irish situation came, interestingly enough, from Quebec separatists who saw echoes of their own 'struggle' in the cause of Irish nationalism. Quebec, after all, had also been conquered by the English, its language and culture placed *under siege*, and its *right to self-determination* undermined by the Anglo-Protestant establishment. And Quebec's Catholics, like Ireland's, had refused to fight

Britain's imperial wars, and had tried to make the best of the status quo until it simply became unbearable. In modern times, the Parti Quebecoi's foray into the Ulster situation came during the hunger strikes of 1981, when it agreed to help finance Bernadette Devlin's visit to Canada on condition that members of the PQ could meet with her. "The general level of support in terms of trade unions and the PQ," admitted Devlin, "is very important to us in the H Block." As for the political future of Quebec she stated: "There are many similarities of a developing nationalist movement, and the end of the situation has to be an independent Quebec." A PQ spokesman, after meeting Devlin, apparently disagreed. "The situation in Ireland is very particular," he concluded, "very different from the situation in Quebec." To the knowledge of this author there was no further official contact between the PQ and Irish republicans, although Devlin did revisit Quebec in 1984.[181]

It is uncertain why the PQ suddenly went cold on Irish nationalism, but one explanation is that inviting comparisons with Northern Ireland was not really in the PQ's interests. If Quebec nationalists wished to give the impression that separation would be a painless, orderly process then it was best to keep the Irish precedent at arms length. Better to focus on the likes of Norway. After all, Quebec had a sizeable anglophone minority who insisted that regardless of the result of any referendum on separation, they weren't going anywhere. If Quebec had to be partitioned in order to ensure their right to remain Canadian, so be it. If Canada was divisible so was Quebec. Areas along the Ontario border would remain with Canada, as would the jewel in the crown, Montreal. Echoes of Ulster 1912. Better leave well enough alone.

There is another important reason for the willingness of Canadian politicians to avoid interfering in Ulster. That is the fact that Canada's "large number of citizens of Irish descent" referred to by the *Globe* were, by the late 1960s, hardly Irish at all, and were as baffled by the whole situation as most others. One is hard pressed to overstate the extent to which the Irish Catholic experience in late 20th century Canada has diverged from that of the United States. Irish Canadians, it can be safely stated, quickly become mere Canadians. Some came to develop an affection for the British link, some merely came to accept the crown and empire as part and parcel of Canada's constitutional status. Whatever the case, the phenomenon of 'Irish Americanism' was never reproduced in Canada. With minor exceptions, the Irish communities' political leaders, and the Roman Catholic Church, actively encouraged this metamorphosis. D'Arcy McGee, one-time Irish rebel turned Father of Confederation, admonished Canada's Irish to leave Ireland's troubles behind them in Ireland. Today there is no longer an Irish lobby worth mentioning. The Catholic Church, the entity to which Irishmen had given custody of their identity, is now as culturally diverse as the country itself, and Poles, Italians, and Filipinos have long since overthrown Irish predominance. Once the church's powerbrokers, they are now one group among many, and their numbers steadily decline. The Saint Patrick's Day parades every March, although extremely well attended, are family affairs, where 'everyone is Irish for a day', political content is non-existent, and Canadians with emphatically non-Irish names leap at another opportunity to drown their late winter blues in jugs of beer. In terms of ethnic consciousness, Irish Canadians don't have much of an existence at all, or care much about Ireland, North or South. It is, to them, very much a foreign country. There is no pro-Sinn Fein element worth noting. There is no Ted Kennedy to run the tricolour up the flagpole in pursuit of the Irish vote, if for no other reason than there is no longer an Irish vote--at least not in the sense of there being an organised, self-consciously 'Irish' element to be appeased.[182] There's a Ukrainian vote, the women's vote, the gay vote, the protest vote--but no Irish vote. It is perhaps Canada's most remarkable case of cultural assimilation. One only has to think of former prime minister Brian Mulroney, an Irish Catholic by descent, referring to the British monarchy as a Canadian institution, and to himself as a monarchist. There is also the sight of Canada's many St. Patrick's Day parades, where the Union Jack is carried alongside the tricolour, and any and all political content whatsoever is barred from the day's proceedings.[183]

Now, having said this, there have been a handful of occasions where Irish nationalists have found supporters in Canada among Irish-born Canadians. There is a pro-Sinn Fein organisation in Toronto which, however small, attempts to promote the republican cause. It is also a certainty that the IRA has received at least a trickle of weapons from sympathisers in Canada, and occasionally a Royal visitor is greeted by a handful of protesters. But that's it. No riots, no marches, and precious little press coverage from a Canadian media that has been, without exception, hostile to everything the IRA represents. True, at the beginning of the troubles there was the occasional sympathetic editorial,[184] but as soon as the complexity of the Ulster situation became clear, and the unremitting violence of the IRA continued to shock public opinion, the republican cause lost all support. Canada, as Mao would have put it, was one unaccommodating pool for IRA fish.

Nor, it should be mentioned, is there any longer a significant Orange element to be appeased, or, for that matter, to be reacted against. The old cultural and political links to Ulster are gone. The parade of the Loyal Orange Association that takes place every 'Twelfth', although colourful, is now one of Toronto's smaller annual parades. It fades in terms of size and popularity with Caribana, the Santa Claus parade, or, ironically, the St. Patrick's Day parade.[185] With approximately 1000-1500 participants it proceeds from Queens Park down Yonge Street, past countless Irish gift shops, to the Anglican St. James Cathedral. Here the Canadian and British anthems are sung, and off they go for lunch. Next week they'll gather in Perry Sound for another parade, and, with the exception of a few cameo appearances (the Santa Claus parade for example) that's the parade season done for. The situation in Vancouver is much the same.

No longer do politicians, great or small, feel the slightest need or desire to join an Orange lodge to ensure their election. Nor do considerable numbers of Canadians of Ulster ancestry take an active interest in the fate of Ulster's Protestants. When Northern Ireland's Orangemen kick their marching season into high gear each summer, most Canadians simply look on in disinterest or puzzled detachment. 'What's an Orangeman?', asked a young lady at an Ontario library when I asked to see the current edition of the *Orange Sentinel*. Unfortunately for the Order, it's an organisation whose day, at least as a Canadian institution, has passed. Indeed, the Toronto and Vancouver Orange parades carry on essentially because the Orange Lodge has again become an Irish, or, more correctly, an Ulster, institution. Simply put, the main element keeping the Orange parade going in Toronto and Vancouver is the steady flow of Ulster émigrés to Ontario and British Columbia. Even the accents give away the new ethnic nature of Canadian Orangeism, as do the small gatherings of persons following the parade waving their 'Red Hand of Ulster' flags and shouting the Sash. This change can also be seen in the age disparity between the bands and marchers. The older folks in the parade are mostly of Canadian birth, and probably not even of Ulster ancestry. The younger marchers are largely Ulster immigrants, or the children of Ulster immigrants, and it is they who give the parade its energy. It is they who draw the followers on the sidewalk and who issue the occasional cry of 'No Surrender' or, more profanely, 'Kick the Pope'. And it is certain individuals among them that have secured the trickle of arms to loyalist paramilitaries in Northern Ireland, not native-born Canadians. Canadian-born Protestants have long since abandoned the Lodge. What remains is a small ethnic organisation of little influence and, outside of a handful of rural communities, of no political clout.

Nor do Canada's Protestant churches, which have lost their commanding position within English-speaking Canada, care much about Ireland. Not only has their 'share' of the Canadian population dropped significantly since 1945, but the major denominations are increasingly multicultural in composition. The largest churches are also unapologetically ecumenical and inclusive. Their modern concerns, moreover, are less those of protecting the gains of the Reformation, or even preparing souls for the Judgement Day, than in addressing social ills in the here and now. Self-questioning is at the core of modern day Canadian Protestantism. It no longer sings the praises of Anglo-Saxon mission, and freely admits to the wrongs imposed on others by that same sense of mission. The rights of the poor, visible minorities, women, refugees, the masses of oppressed in the third world, and even the environment hold the attention of modern-day Protestantism. True, there are islands of fundamentalism in Canada, but they exist at the fringes of society, not at its heart. The Northern Ireland conflict, therefore, is baffling and offensive to most Canadian Christians. The church press has offered little comment on the conflict, except to occasionally note efforts of Protestants and Catholics attempting to work together for peace. Kinder and gentler Christians! Other reports were factual and very brief, such as the Presbyterian Record's noting of a meeting of the General Assembly of the Presbyterian Church in Ireland.[186] Canada's Christians, Protestants and Catholics alike, had moved on.

--Chapter Ten--

THE ULSTER PEACE PROCESS (1994-)

On October 20th, 1998, a remarkable thing occurred in Ottawa which, a year or two earlier, would have been unthinkable. Gerry Adams, president of the IRA-allied Sinn Fein party, received a standing ovation in the Canadian House of Commons. Earlier in the day he had met with Canada's prime minister, Jean Chretien, and foreign minister, Lloyd Axworthy. While parliament was sitting, Chretien had pointed Adams out in the visitor's gallery and the House rose in applause. Given the traditional attitude of the Canadian establishment to Sinn Fein and the IRA, this was a remarkable development indeed. Adams represented a political tradition which, since the days of the Fenian Raids and beyond, had been anathematized by the Canadian establishment and public opinion alike. On several occasions Adams himself had been denied access to Canada and had once been detained trying to enter Canada at Vancouver Airport. As far as Canada was concerned, Adams was a spokesman for terrorism and therefore unwelcome in Canada. And yet here he was, in October of 1998, receiving a standing ovation from Canadian parliamentarians. What happened? This final chapter will briefly examine the significant political developments within Ireland since the IRA's cease-fire of 1994, and the Canadian response to these developments.

THE SEARCH FOR PEACE

In December of 1993 the British and Irish premiers, John Major and Albert Reynolds, released a framework document outlining the principles which must guide any resolution of the Ulster conflict. John Major reaffirmed that the British government was dedicated to upholding the democratic wish of the greater number of the people of Northern Ireland on the issue of Irish unification. On this basis, he reiterated that the British government had no selfish strategic or economic interest in Northern Ireland. Its primary interest was to see peace, stability and reconciliation established by agreement among all the people who inhabited Ireland, and committed itself to work together with the Irish government to achieve such an agreement. The role of the British government would be "to encourage, facilitate and enable" a settlement based on full respect for the rights and identities of both traditions in Ireland. It accepted that such an agreement may take the form of agreed structures for the island as a whole, including a united Ireland. It was, however, for the "people of Ireland alone," by agreement between the two parts respectively, to exercise their right to bring about a united Ireland, if that was their wish. It reaffirmed that, in such circumstances, it would introduce the necessary legislation to give effect to this.

For his part, the Irish prime minister acknowledged that the lessons of Irish history, and especially of Northern Ireland, showed that stability and well-being could not be found under any political system which is refused allegiance or rejected on grounds of identity by a significant minority of those governed by it. For this reason, it was wrong to attempt to impose a united Ireland in the absence of the freely given consent of a majority of the people of Northern Ireland. He accepted, therefore, on behalf of the Irish government, that "the democratic right of self-determination by the people of Ireland as a whole must be achieved and exercised with and subject to the agreement and consent of a majority of the people of Northern Ireland," and must, consistent with justice and equity, respect the democratic dignity, civil rights and religious liberties of both communities.

Both governments accepted that Irish unity would be achieved only by those who favored this outcome persuading those who did not, peacefully and without coercion or violence, that this was the best future. Once this was achieved both governments would pass the necessary legislation bringing a united Ireland into effect. But regardless of the will of the majority, the old divisions within the British Isles had to come to an end. There was to be no going back to the days when inherited grievances were allowed to dominate Anglo-Irish relations. The Declaration reiterated that the development of Europe, of itself, would require new approaches to serve interests common to both parts of Ireland, and to Ireland and the UK. Within these realities the people of Northern Ireland were free to determine their own future.[187]

Although the Downing Street Declaration did little more than reiterate the principles underlining the Anglo-Irish Agreement of 1985, it had a pointed message for the republican movement. Your quarrel is not with the British state, but with Ulster unionists--fellow Irishmen! Britain had no economic or strategic interests in Ireland. If Irishmen could agree to a united Ireland, Britain would gladly step aside. But a united Ireland was out of the question without the support of the majority of Northern Ireland's electorate. To that extent the political violence of the IRA was counter-productive, and only served to polarize attitudes.

Republicans had, of course, heard this message before. It had been put to them in 1987 when John Hume, leader of the constitutional nationalist SDLP party, held private talks with Gerry Adams. He reminded Adams that he and his party also sought a united Ireland, but that violence was wrong. Not only was it morally indefensible, but it was counter-productive. Contrary to republican ideology, the British were not holding onto Ulster for strategic advantage, or holding it *for NATO*. In the age of intercontinental missiles, Northern Ireland held no strategic value for Britain whatsoever. As for British economic interests in Ireland, what were they? Every thinking person knew that Northern Ireland was a major drain on the British exchequer, an economic black hole from which London dearly wished to extract itself. If Britain could honorably withdraw from Northern Ireland without appearing to abandon the unionists, or succumb to terrorism, then it would gladly do so. If Sinn Fein wanted the Brits out, it was in their interest to comprehend that the Brits also wanted out, but that it wasn't going to happen without majority support from within Northern Ireland itself. To continue the war, therefore, only served to prolong the suffering. (And besides, if the experts were correct there would be a Catholic majority in Northern Ireland by 2050. A united Ireland could then conceivably be voted into existence.) This message, delivered in 1987 by the SDLP, took several years to sink in with the republican leadership. By 1994, however, senior republicans, and Adams in particular, were coming around to this reasoning.

Another major factor contributing to the re-think within Sinn Fein and the IRA was the sheer exhaustion of the republican movement. For all their violence, and their willingness to endure and inflict suffering, their goal of a united Ireland was no closer than it had been in 1969. Thousands of people had been killed or wounded, hundreds of republicans were doing life sentences in British and Irish jails, and countless children were growing up without fathers or the prospect of decent employment. Moreover, for all their complaints about the social depravation of the nationalist community, republicans were increasingly aware that no factor damaged Catholics' economic prospects quite like the IRA's campaign. It was one thing to ask the nationalist community to make such sacrifices in the short term, but, after a quarter century of violence, victory seemed no closer. On top of this, republican violence was increasingly being matched by loyalist violence, bringing greater hardship to the community the IRA claimed it was *defending*.

Several outrages against civilian targets, whether intentional or accidental, had also done serious damage to the IRA's claim that it was fighting a just war. Throughout the Troubles the IRA was an organization attuned to the skills of propaganda. To bomb an Army barracks or shoot a judge could be portrayed to the international media as a struggle against an oppressive system, and that the IRA only targeted those actively involved in upholding that system. In 1987, however, an IRA bomb killed eleven Protestant civilians at a Remembrance Day ceremony. Over the next several years many other non-combatants would be killed, from English school children to grocers who 'assisted' the occupation forces by delivering milk to police stations. Under pressure from the security forces, the IRA's definition of a legitimate target had been stretched to include any individual who did any business whatsoever with a branch of the security forces. When an IRA bomb, planted in a busy shopping district in the summer of 1994, killed another nine Protestants civilians, the republican movement had reached its lowest ebb. World opinion was increasingly viewing them as ruthless sectarian thugs, hopelessly addicted to violence.

All of these factors were bearing down on the republican movement when, in August of 1994, the IRA announced an open-ended cease-fire. Gerry Adams was pivotal in securing that cease-fire. For over a year and a half he and other senior republicans had been in secret contact with the British government, attempting to negotiate an honorable way out of the conflict. When the cease-fire was announced every observer knew that there were many republicans who saw it as a betrayal of the cause. Many argued, therefore, that government policy should be to encourage and flatter that element, led by Adams, which was willing to make violence a thing of the past. In the months and years ahead, Gerry Adams and other senior republicans would not only be invited to Downing Street, but to the White House. The objective, in part, was to bring the republican movement in from the cold. A prolonged period of peace would make it extremely difficult for the IRA to return to war. More significantly, to be wined and dined in the White House, and proclaimed by the press as a great peacemaker, made it difficult for Adams to permit a return to violence. The image of senior republicans being greeted as statesmen in the halls of power, moreover, had immense propaganda value.

Gerry Adams, who had been among the first republicans to realize the possibilities of 'political' as opposed to 'armed' struggle, was pivotal in convincing other republicans that, in the short term, they would have to settle for something less than a united Ireland. In April of 1998, therefore, Adams was a signatory to the Good Friday Agreement that accepted the reality of

Northern Ireland's position within the United Kingdom. It was a dangerous step to take. As noted in chapter 5, when the IRA leader, Michael Collins, accepted in 1921 that compromise was necessary and signed the Anglo-Irish Treaty creating an Irish dominion in southern Ireland, as opposed to an all-Ireland republic, it prompted the outbreak of civil war. IRA factions turned against one another. Collins himself was ambushed and killed by his former colleagues. Today, as in 1921, there are republican militarists who are resolved on continuing the armed struggle. In October of 1998 a bomb, planted by republican dissidents, exploded in the city of Omagh killing 29 civilians. Gerry Adams, who had never once denounced IRA actions in the past, denounced the Omagh bombing "unequivocally." Interested observers were determined that Adams not lose his nerve.

It was undoubtedly in part to encourage him that he was applauded in the House of Commons. Some weeks before, John Hume and David Trimble, leader of the Ulster Unionist Party, had been awarded a Nobel Peace Prize for their efforts in securing the Good Friday compromise. Some critics had been adamant that other participants should also have shared the award. British premier Tony Blair, Irish premier Bertie Ahern, and Britain's Northern Ireland secretary, Mo Mowlam, were among those named. Some had been adamant that Gerry Adams should also have shared the award, given the risks he was taking for peace. It was well known that many within Sinn Fein believed he should have shared the award. Some press reports suggested that the Nobel committee had actually considered expanding the number of persons honored by the award, but refrained from doing so for one persuasive reason: no British politician, and certainly no Ulster unionist, could have jointly accepted a peace award with a spokesman for the Irish Republican Army. It was essential, however, that the Sinn Fein leadership not become demoralized or develop a sense of being held in contempt.

Canada, moreover, had a stake in the success of the peace process. Clifford Shearing, head of the

University of Toronto's criminology centre, was an advisor to the Patton Commission looking into the highly emotional issue of police reform in Northern Ireland. Another Canadian, Chief Justice William Hoyt of the New Brunswick Supreme Court, is part of a three-person team reexamining the events surrounding Bloody Sunday in 1972. Most importantly, as stated in the introduction to this book, General John de Chastelain, former Chief of Staff of the Canadian Armed Forces, was actually co-chairing the whole process in Northern Ireland. He was also the head of the body responsible for securing the decommissioning of all paramilitary weapons, the most contentious part of the entire peace process. The success of the peace process, therefore, would bring a certain honor to Canada. And many politicians with a sense of history would surely have thought it just that Canada, which in earlier generations was so intimately involved in the Irish Question, should now be involved in its solution.

The prospects for Canadian investment in a new and peaceful Northern Ireland would also have encouraged parliamentarians to embrace Adams' peace overtures. Canada, after all, was one of the largest sources of international investment in the Irish Republic, and Bombardier Inc., the Montreal-based aerospace company, which provides 7000 jobs at Belfast's Shorts aircraft plant, is currently Northern Ireland's largest private-sector employer. With the possibility of peace breaking out in Ulster comes the possibility of greater investment in an English-speaking market previously tapped into only by the brave. Possibly the prime minister, among others, hoped that the successful resolution of the Ulster conflict within existing constitutional boundaries would also send a powerful message to Quebec separatists. If such blood enemies as Irish Catholics and Irish Protestants could agree to share the same house, no less could be expected of Canadians. Perhaps for this reason Jean Charest, leader of Quebec's Liberal Party, could be found giving a stridently pro-federalist lecture at Belfast's Queens University, and Jean Chretien would become the first Canadian prime minister to visit Northern Ireland since John Diefenbaker in 1961.[188]

Quebec separatists also had reason to welcome Adams to Canada. Both Irish Catholics and French Canadians had, after all, labored under the injustices, both real and imagined, of British colonialism. They had both been the target of Orange anti-Catholicism and distrust of anything that was not British and Protestant. In more secular times both communities have had to struggle against the new imperialism of the English language and the onslaught of Anglo-American culture. While Sinn Fein remained wedded to the armed struggle, however, Quebec separatists' common cause with Irish nationalism remained muted. Since the cease-fire, however, Sinn Fein has been embraced by many separatists as fellow travelers in the cause of national freedom. In March of 1999, to acknowledge St. Patrick's Day, the Saint Jean Baptiste Society, a prominent Quebec nationalist organisation, placed a notice in the Montreal Gazette congratulating Irish nationalists on their long struggle towards nationhood. French Canadians were also engaged in a long struggle to win freedom, and the St. Jean Baptiste Society wished godspeed to the Irish cause. Such a notice could never have been issued while the Irish nationalist 'struggle' included the IRA.

For those Canadians who genuinely wished to see reconciliation in Northern Ireland, however, beyond a mere ceasation of hostilities, there was little cause for optimism. Indeed, since the signing of the Good Friday Agreement in April of 1998 relations between unionists and nationalists in Ulster had deteriorated markedly. The IRA had stated categorically on several occasions that it had no intention of decommissioning, and had rejected appeals for it to announce that its war was over. Unionists were furious over British compromises on policing, the public display of flags, and the right to parade. The nomination of Martin McGuinness, a former commander in the Derry IRA, to the Northern Ireland executive was seen by many as a compromise too far. Nationalists were also incensed by the ongoing 'siege' of a Catholic community near Portadown after it refused to allow an Orange parade to continue down a route it had used for two centuries. Intermittent violence by loyalist dissidents had also embittered many Catholics who saw the government's insistence on IRA decommissioning as one-sided and biased. Unionists responded that the loyalist dissidents weren't about to enter government. Sinn Fein was, and therein lay the fundamental difference. No cabinet minister could have access to a private, fully armed militia. When the Northern Ireland executive met for the first time in December of 1999, David Trimble was on record as stating that the IRA had two months to begin delivering weapons. If General de Chastelain could not produce 'product' by February 1st, the Ulster Unionist Party would withdraw from the executive. This it did.

As the second anniversary of the Good Friday Agreement approached, the political situation in Ulster seemed bleak. May 22nd was also the date set out in the Agreement for the completion of IRA decommissioning. Many unionists held that if the IRA had not even begun disarming by then, or given any indication that it planned to disarm at some point in the future, then the Agreement was nullified. In early May, however, the IRA stunned most observers, including many republicans, by announcing that it would open several of its arms bunkers to international observation. While it did not state that the war was over, or offer to hand in weapons, many observers believed that it was a significant development. The IRA, it appeared, was crossing its Rubicon. Allowing international observers to regularly examine IRA dumps, to ensure that no weapons had been used, was not the action of an Army preparing itself for renewed hostilities. If nothing else it was a huge confidence-building measure that many moderate unionists believed deserved to be acknowledged. On May 27th, therefore, despite the objections of a vociferous minority, the Ulster Unionist Party voted to return to government with Sinn Fein.

CONCLUSION

The applause offered to Gerry Adams in the Canadian House of Commons was a momentous event. In the recent past, the House of Commons was an unlikely venue for a member of Sinn Fein to be let into, let alone given a standing ovation in. In one sense, however, it was perhaps fitting that the president of Sinn Fein, once he had turned his back on militant republicanism, should be welcomed in Canada's parliament. After all, on the lawn of that building stood a statue of another former Irish republican rebel, Thomas D'Arcy McGee. Not only did McGee renounce his extremist creed and develop an attachment to the British parliamentary system. He also encouraged Irish nationalists to further their interests through exclusively peaceful and constitutional means. Although Gerry Adams' remains an Irish republican, and still refers to the IRA as 'freedom fighters', his path from militarism to parliamentarianism has its parallels with McGee's own transformation. Like D'Arcy McGee, Gerry Adams is now willing to pursue politics through constitutional means. Whether his fate will also resemble that of D'Arcy McGee and Michael Collins—-assassinated by dissident republicans for their betrayal of the Irish cause--only time will tell.

One thing is certain. It is fitting that Canada should be actively involved in what one hopes is the final stage of Ireland's long Troubles. Canadians had been active in the quest for a settlement for almost eighty years. From the earliest years of the Home Rule movement until Eire's decision to proclaim itself a republic and leave the commonwealth, Canadians had actively sought a way to reconcile Irish nationalism with membership in the British commonwealth. Although Canadian interest, both public and official, dwindled after 1949, the year Eire became a republic, and the violence that overtook Ulster twenty years later further served to alienate Canadians from Ireland, it is fitting that, in the wake of peace, Canadians are again involved in securing a permanent and just settlement in Ireland. Both Northern Ireland and Canada, after all, contain "two nations struggling" within the confines of one state. In a rapidly changing world, there is perhaps still room for both countries to learn from the experience of the other.

ENDNOTES

CHAPTER ONE

[1] William Gladstone, cited in *Hansard*, House of Commons Debates, Ottawa, 4 May 1886, col. 1024.

[2] *Hansard*, House of Commons Debates, Ottawa, 1882, p.1034

[3] Ibid.

[4] Ibid., p.1035

[5] Ibid., p.1043

[6] Ibid., pp.1039-1044

[7] Ibid., p.1043

[8] Ibid.

[9] "'Wrongs of Ireland': The Home Rule Question Reviewed by Professor Goldwin Smith," *Orange Sentinel*, 27 May 1886; *Irish History and Irish Character*, J.H. and Jas Parker, Oxford and London, 1862; and, "The Greatness of England," *The Contemporary Review*, vol.34, 1878-79.

[10] "British Affairs," *The Week*, 7 October 1886

[11] Goldwin Smith, *Dismemberment No Remedy*, London, 1886, p.15

[12] "The Imperial Veto Ineffectual," *The Week*, February 25, 1886

[13] Smith, *Dismemberment No Remedy*, p.17

[14] "The Act of Union: True Relation of the Land of the Shamrock to the Land of the Rose," *Orange Sentinel*, 25 March 1886

[15] *Reminiscences by Goldwin Smith (Arnold Haultain,ed.)*, Macmillan, New York, 1910, p.317

[16] G.S. to Professor Tyndall, Toronto, November 10, 1885, *A Selection from Goldwin Smith's Correspondence Comprising Letters Chiefly to and from his English Friends, Between the Years 1846 and 1910 (Arnold Haultain,ed.)*, McClelland and Goodchild, Toronto, 1913, p.180

[17] G.S. to Lord Farrer, Toronto, January 14, 1883, *A Selection from Goldwin Smith's Correspondence*, p.144

[18] "St. Patrick's Day," *The Week*, 25 March 1886

[19] untitled, *Toronto Telegram*, 9 March 1886

[20] "The Loyalist Demonstration," *Orange Sentinel*, 9 March 1886

[21] untitled, *Toronto Telegram*, 9 March 1886

[22] untitled, *Canada Presbyterian*, 19 May 1886

[23] Ibid.

CHAPTER TWO

[24] At a meeting in December of 1890, 45 of his fellow Irish MPs withdrew their support from his leadership. At a subsequent meeting Parnell was formally deposed, being replaced by Justin McCarthy.

[25] Parnell died October 1891

[26] "The Irish Party," *Toronto Globe*, 19 November 1890

[27] "Tried in the Balance," *Victoria Daily Colonist*, 4 December 1890

[28] "Repudiated," *Victoria Daily Colonist*, 3 December 1890

[29] "Our Modern Knight," *Vancouver Daily World*, 20 June 1892

[30] *The Blake Demonstration*, Toronto, 1892, p.14

[31] "The Blake Demonstration," *Toronto Globe*, 20 September 1892

[32] "The Offer to Blake," *Ottawa Citizen*, 16 June 1892

[33] "Mr. Blake's Welcome Home," *Ottawa Evening Journal*, 21 September 1892

[34] "Mr. Blake's Reception," *Toronto World*, 15 September 1892

[35] "In Defence of Empire," *Toronto World*, 21 September 1892

[36] "The Anti-Home Rule Meeting," *Toronto Globe*, 21 September 1892

CHAPTER THREE

[37] "Canada and Irish Affairs," *Canadian Annual Review for 1903*, p.334

[38] "The Irish Land Bill," *Winnipeg Free Press*, 4 April 1903

[39] untitled, *Orange Sentinel*, 28 September 1911

[40] "Canada and the Irish Home Rule Question," *Canadian Annual Review* for 1912, p.143

[41] untitled, *Toronto Evening Telegram*, 11 July 1914

[42] "Canada and the Irish Home Rule Question," pp.143-44

[43] Ibid., p.143

[44] "The Ulster Division," *Orange Sentinel*, 3 August 1916

[45] untitled, *Orange Sentinel*, 4 May 1916

[46] Carl Berger, *The Sense of Power: Studies in the Ideas of Canadian Imperialism, 1867-1914*, University of Toronto Press, 1970, p.71

[47] W.M. Baker, "A Case Study of Anti-Americanism in English-Speaking Canada: The Election Campaign of 1911," *Canadian Historical Review*, 1970, p.432

[48] "Saturday's Orange Demonstration," *Orange Sentinel*, 13 July 1914

[49] "The Greatest Parade Ever," *Toronto Evening Telegram*, 13 July 1914

[50] "Parade Biggest and Most Serious Ever," *Toronto Daily Star*, 13 July 1914

[51] "The Twelfth Celebrations," *Toronto World*, 13 July 1914

[52] "The Grey County Orange Celebrations," *Toronto Globe*, 13 July 1914

[53] *Hansard*, House of Commons, Ottawa, 27 March 1914

[54] Ibid., 20 March 1914

[55] Ibid., 12 May 1914

[56] untitled, *Daily Mail and Empire*, 13 July 1914. It should be noted that the Orange Lodge had offered active support for unionist resistance in previous years. In March of 1893, for example, N.C. Wallace, the Grand Master of British North America, and Comptroller for Customs in the Conservative government, had stated the following of unionist intentions at an Orange rally in Kingston.

> They are preparing for action. Their unalterable determination is never to submit to Home Rule, and they will have the sympathy of the Orangemen of Canada--aye more than sympathy! they shall have our active aid if that active aid be necessary. (*Globe* 18 March 1893)

In 1893, however, such action was largely rhetorical given the Lords' resolve to veto any bill passed by the House of Commons. By 1914, however, with the abolition of the Lords' veto, the 'threat' had suddenly become more serious.

[57] "Ulster," *Daily Mail and Empire*, 30 September 1912

[58] "The Irish Question," *Toronto Star*, 6 July 1914

[59] "The Irish Difficulty," *Toronto Daily Star*, 9 July 1914

[60] "An Untenable Position," *Toronto Globe*, 10 July 1914

[61] "Editorial Notes," *Nanaimo Free Press*, 30 September 1912

[62] "A Burlesque With Tragic Possibilities," *Victoria Daily Times*, 28 September 1912

[63] "Ulster--What Convulsed Her?," *Toronto World*, 18 September 1912

[64] "Spectator's Comments and Notes of Public Interest," *Canadian Churchman*, 18 April 1912

[65] "Should Stop Meddling," *Victoria Daily Times*, 14 July 1912

[66] George Denison, *The Struggle for Imperial Unity*, London, 1909, p.69

[67] *Hansard, House of Commons Debates*, Ottawa, 27 March 1914

CHAPTER FOUR

[68] "Canadians and Ireland," *Toronto Globe*, 1 June 1920

[69] "America and the Irish Question," *The Statesman*, 7 February 1920

[70] "A Worthless Report," *Hamilton Spectator*, 4 April 1921

[71] "Church Protests," *Calgary Herald*, 23 December 1919

[72] "The Twelfth in Ireland," *Charlottetown Examiner*, 15 July 1920

[73] "The Situation in Ireland," *Presbyterian Witness* (Toronto), 27 January 1921

[74]. "No 'Irish Parliament'," *Guelph Evening Mercury*, 9 April 1921

[75] See, for example, "An Irish Republic," *London Free Press,* 13 February 1920

[76] "Public Reception Given to the Ulster Delegates," *Toronto Globe,* 12 February 1920; "Wild Welcome by Orangemen at the Orange Headquarters," *Orange Sentinel,* 19 February 1920. For the enthusiasm with which the delegates' message was being received also see "The Irish Problem," *Empire Club Speeches*, February 1920

[77] "The Truth About Ireland," *Christian Guardian,* 11 February 1920

[78] "No Solution in Ireland Possible," *Maclean's Magazine,* March 1919

[79] "Breeders of Strife," *Toronto Globe,* 9 June 1920

[80] "The Irish Appeal to the U.S. Congress," *Presbyterian Witness* (Halifax), 8 March 1919

[81] See, for example, "Ulster Self-Determination," *Vancouver Province,* 19 May 1921; "The Irish Question in the U.S.A.," *Presbyterian Record,* May 1920

[82] "The Sinn Fein Movement," *Presbyterian Witness* (Halifax), 1 February 1919

[83] See, for example, "Insidious Propaganda," *Victoria Daily Colonist*, 10 December 1920

[84] See, for example, "Angling for the Irish Vote," *Regina Morning Leader*, 3 June 1920

[85] "The Big Two and Their Two Big Problems," *Toronto World,* 23 December 1918

[86] "Canada Should Be Prepared For Grave Possibilities," *Orange Sentinel,* 20 May 1920

[87] John A. Stewart, "World Conspiracy Against Anglo-American Friendship," *Empire Club of Canada, Addresses Delivered To The Members During the Year 1920*, Warwick Bros. and Rutter Limited, Toronto, 1920, p.92

[88] See, for example, "The Grave Dangers of Peace—Germany is Still Making War By Propaganda," *Macleans Magazine,* January 1919; "Soviets in Touch With Sinn Fein Evidence Shows," *Vancouver Daily Province,* 22 April 1921; "Soviets Aid Republicans in Ireland," *Manitoba Free Press,* 11 May 1921.

[89] "Church Protests," *Calgary Herald,* 23 December 1919

[90] "From Week to Week," *Canadian Churchman*, 6 May 1920

[91] "Attacking the Empire," *Christian Guardian*, 22 December 1920

[92] "Canada and Ireland," *Canadian Annual Review*, 1921, p.309

[93] "Our Imperialized School System," *The Statesman*, 17 April 1920

[94] "Irish Ingratitude," *Catholic Register*, 1 May 1919

[95] *The Statesman* 29 January 1921; cited in "Canada and Ireland," *Canadian Annual Review*, 1921, p.306

[96] "Ireland and Canadian Imperialism," *The Statesman*, 15 May 1920

[97] "Another Attack on the Flag," *Kingston British Whig*, 12 March 1921

[98] "Canada and Ireland," p.308

[99] "Crawford Will Try No More Meetings," *Vancouver Daily Province*, 28 April 1921

CHAPTER FIVE

[100] Cited in John A. Murphy's "The Anglo-Irish Treaty and After: The Canadian Model and Context," *The Untold Story: The Irish in Canada*, Celtic Arts of Canada, Toronto, 1987, p. 887

[101] See, for example, "Dominion Home Rule," *Ottawa Journal*, 7 May 1921

[102] "New Hope for Ireland," *Presbyterian Witness* (Toronto), 21 July 1921

[103] "The New Dominion," *Canadian Historical Review*, September 1923, p.894

[104] "Ireland and the Treaty," *Toronto Mail and Empire*, 21 January 1922

[105] Ibid.

[106] J.A. Strahan, "The Position and Prospects of Ulster," *Dalhousie Review*, 1925

CHAPTER SIX

[107] Thomas D'Arcy McGee, *The Irish Position in British and in Republican North America*, M. Longmoore and Co. Printing House, Montreal, 1866, p.6

[108] Cited in R. Burns, "D'Arcy McGee and the Fenians," M. Harmon, ed., *Fenians and Fenianism*, University of Washington Press, Seattle, 1970, p.87

[109] Ibid., p.86

[110] "The Threatened Fenian Raid," *The Canadian Freeman*, 11 June 1868

[111] "Give Ireland What Canada Has," *Irish Canadian*, 2 September 1868

[112] "The Home Rulers Dine," *Toronto World*, 17 March 1886

[113] Archives of Ontario, *Charles J. Foy Papers* [National Vice President of the Ancient Order of Hibernians, Canada.], File 14

[114] *Catholic Register*, 10 September, 13 August 1914

[115] "Pax Britannica," Catholic Register, 17 September 1914

[116] John O'Connor, *Letters of John O'Connor, M.P. on Fenianism: addressed to His Excellency the Right Honourable John Young, P.C., G.C.B., G.C.MG., governor-general of Canada*, Toronto, 1870, p.1

[117] "Give Ireland What Canada Has," *Irish Canadian*, 2 September 1868

[118] untitled, *Catholic Register*, 1 March 1917

[119] "Ireland's Parliament," *Catholic Record*, 26 March 1914

[120] *Charles J. Foy Papers*, File 14

[121] untitled, *Catholic Register*, 27 April 1916

[122] "The Dublin Outrage," *Globe*, 26 April 1916

[123] untitled, Catholic Register, 27 May 1916

[124] "Egyptian Bondage," *Catholic Register*, 17 April 1919

[125] "Irish Ingratitude," *Catholic Register*, 1 May 1919

[126] "Repudiated," *Catholic Register*, 14 November 1918

[127] "Canadian-Irish Opinions and Action," *Canadian Annual Review for 1919*, p.236

[128] "Canadians and Ireland," *Toronto Globe*, 1 June 1920

[129] "Ulster and the Orange Order in Canada," *Canadian Annual Review for 1921*, pp.313-14

[130] "Greenwood and the Irish Question," *Toronto Star*, 10 April 1920

[131] cited in "Canadian Relations With Irish Affairs," *Canadian Annual Review for 1922*, pp.194-6

CHAPTER SEVEN

[132] *Hansard*, House of Commons Debates, Ottawa, 31 March 1903, col.763

[133] S.W. Horall, *Canada and the Irish Question: A Study of the Canadian Response to Irish Home Rule 1882-1893*, MA thesis, Carleton University, Ottawa, 1966, pp.11-14

[134] Ibid., p.15

[135] Ibid., pp.12-17

[136] Ibid., pp.60-75

[137] Ibid., pp.106-110

[138] Ibid., pp.110-119

[139] Mark Gowan, "The De-Greening of the Irish: Toronto's Irish Catholic Press, Imperialism, and the Forging of a New Identity, 1887-1914," *Historical Papers*, Canadian Catholic Historical Association, Ottawa, 1978, p.102

[140] Horall, pp.120-136

[141] Ibid., pp.137-141

[142] Ibid., pp.43-59

[143] Ibid., p.43

[144] Henri Bourassa, *Religion, Langue, Nationalite*, Montreal, 1910. Cited in Joseph Levitt, *Henri Bourassa on Imperialism and Bi-Culturalism, 1900-1918*, Copp Clark Publishing Company, Toronto, 1970, p.128

[145] C.J. Houston and W.J. Smyth, *The Sash Canada Wore: A Historical Geography of the Orange Order in Canada*, University of Toronto Press, Toronto, 1980, p.157

[146] G.S. Kealey, "The Orange Order in Toronto: Religious Riot and the Working Class," R. O'Driscoll and L. Reynolds, eds. *The Untold Story: The Irish in Canada*, Celtic Arts of Canada, Toronto, 1988, p.840

[147] Ramsay Cook, *The Maple Leaf Forever: Essays on Nationalism and Politics in Canada*, Macmillan of Canada, Toronto, 1971, p.71

[148] Carl Berger, *The Sense of Power: Studies in the Ideas of Canadian Imperialism, 1867-1914*, Toronto, 1970; Robert Page, "Canada and the Imperial Idea in the Boer War Years," *Journal of Canadian Studies* 5, 1970; Robert Stamp, "Empire Day in the Schools of Ontario: The Training of Young Imperialists," *Journal of Canadian Studies*, 1973; Matthew R. Bray, "'Fighting as an Ally': The English-Canadian Patriotic Response to the Great War," *Canadian Historical Review* LXI, 2, 1980

[149] George Grant, *Imperial Federation*, Winnipeg Free Press Printers, 1890, p.14

[150] cited in Levitt, *Henri Bourassa on Imperialism and Bi-Culturalism, 1900-1918*, p.164

[151] *Hansard*, House of Commons Debates, Ottawa, 31 March 1903, cols. 778-80

[152] Andre Siegfried, *The Race Question in Canada*, Nash, London, 1907, p.48

[153] "The Self-Determination League for Ireland," *Canadian Annual Review for 1920*, p.309

[154] "Our Imperialized School System," *The Statesman*, 17 April 1920

[155] cited in Levitt, *Henri Bourassa on Imperialism and Bi-Culturalism, 1900-1918*, p.5

CHAPTER EIGHT

[156] "The Irish Boundary Question; Other Countries of the Empire," *Canadian Annual Review for 1925-6*, p.150

[157] "Ireland," *Canadian Annual Review for 1926-27*, p.151

[158] "The Irish Free State," *Canadian Annual Review for the Years 1927-28*, pp.128-9

[159] "Mr. De Valera and Some Realities," *Ottawa Journal*, 26 March 1932

[160] "De Valera in the Saddle," *Victoria Daily Times*, 10 March 1932

[161] "St. Patrick's Day," *Montreal Daily Star*, 16 March 1932

[162] See, for example, *Hansard*, House of Commons Debates, 12 May, 1941, col. 2726

[163] See for example, "A United Christendom," *Globe and Mail*, 8 June 1940

[164] "Britain Wasting No More Time With Dublin," *Montreal Daily Star*, 11 July 1940

[165] "Ireland Alarmed, But Remains Neutral," *Globe*, 11 July 1940

[166] "The Last Neutral," *Vancouver Sun*, 4 May 1945

[167] "'Neutral' Eire," *Macleans*, 1 January 1942

[168] "This Democratic Empire," *Empire Club Speeches*, Toronto, February 1940

[169] "Drive the Snakes Out of Ireland," *Montreal Daily Star*, 10 March 1944

[170] "Absolutely Necessary," *Halifax Herald*, 16 March 1944

[171] "Ireland Breaks Away," Globe and Mail, 18 April 1949

[172] "Ireland Stays Partitioned," *Globe and Mail*, 14 February 1949

CHAPTER NINE

[173] "Government Could Draw on Canadian Experience in Announcing New Initiatives for Ulster," *London Times*, 22 February 1972

[174] John Kenny, The Road to Hillsborough: The Shaping of the Anglo-Irish Agreement, Pergamon Press, New York, 1986, p.50

[175] "Violence Itself Becomes the Irish Cause," *Globe and Mail*, 7 March 1972

[176] "Londonderry Surely Signals Direct Rule for Ulster," *Globe and Mail*, 1 February 1972

[177] "Ulster's 'day of sadness'," *Vancouver Province*, 25 March 1972

[178] With minor exceptions the media has portrayed Great Britain as an 'honest broker' in Northern Ireland, willing to abide by whatever solution the Irish can agree upon. See, for example, "Duty Bound," *Vancouver Sun*, 16 May 1981; "Why Britain is Staying in Ulster," *Winnipeg Free Press*, 1 June 1981

[179] "In Accord on Ulster," *Globe and Mail*, 16 November 1985

[180] "Ireland's Odd Request," *Calgary Herald,* 10 February 1972. Also see, for example, "Canada Refuses Ireland's Plea to Put Pressure on Britain," *Globe and Mail,* 8 February 1972

[181] See "PQ Help 'Important' to Irish Nationalists," *Montreal Gazette,* 18 June 1981; "PQ to Subsidize Irish Nationalist's Tour," *Globe and Mail,* 15 June 1981; "'Suppression' in Quebec Similar to Northern Ireland, Irish Activist Says," *Montreal Gazette,* 31 March 1984

[182] The Canadian media has been extremely critical of American involvement in Northern Ireland. See for example: "Not Their Affair," *Montreal Gazette,* 2 March 1972; "Interference," *Vancouver Sun,* 4 March 1972; "American Irish Blamed for Continuing Violence," *Vancouver Sun,* 15 March 1976; "Fools Rush In," *Globe and Mail,* 29 April 1981; and "Blood Money," *Victoria Times Colonist,* 1 March 1985

[183] "Montreal's Irish Avoid Troubled Politics of Home," *Montreal Gazette,* 17 March 1988; "Irish Nationalists Find There's No Place for Them In The Big Parade," *Montreal Gazette,* 12 March 1991; "Irish Group Stages Protest at Parade," *Globe and Mail,* 20 March 1989

[184] "The Time Has Come," *Catholic Register,* 12 February 1972; "Ireland: The Haves and the Have-Nots," *Catholic Register,* 21 August 1971. Within the same journal, however, there was often very learned pieces such as "Time Runs Out in Ulster," *Catholic Register,* 21 August 1971. By the end of December 1972 the *Register* had come to acknowledge the complexity of the situation, as had other Catholic papers. See for example, "Moderation and Northern Ireland," *Catholic New Times,* 16 May 1981; and "How a Divided Society Imagines Violence," *Catholic New Times,* 14 April 1991

[185] "Toronto City Council Snubs Orangemen Again," *Orange Sentinel,* July/August 1979; "Orange Heyday is Over," *Globe and Mail,* 11 July 1981; "Fading of the Orange," *Globe and Mail,* 12 July 1990; "Parade With a Past: Orange Lodge Marchers Draw Blank Stares," *Globe and Mail,* 15 July 1991

[186] "The General Assembly of the Presbyterian Church in Ireland," *Presbyterian Record*, September 1985

CHAPTER TEN

[187] "The Downing Street Declaration", *Irish Times*, 16 December, 1993
[188] "How the Irish Played a Key Role in the Birth of Quebec", *Celtic Connection*, June 1999

SELECT BIBLIOGRAPHY

Journals, Pamphlets, Articles and Books

Akenson, D.H., "An Agnostic View of the Historiography of the Irish-Americans," *Labour/Le Travail*, 1984

----------- *Being Had: Historians, Evidence, and the Irish in North America*, P.D. Meany, Port Credit,1985

Banks, Margaret, *Edward Blake, Irish Nationalist: A Canadian Statesman in Irish Politics, 1892-1907*, University of Toronto Press, 1957

-------------- "Edward Blake's Relations With Canada During His Irish Career, 1892-1907," *Canadian Historical Review*, March 1954

Baker, W.M., "Squelching the Disloyal Fenian-Sympathizing Brood: T.W. Anglin and Confederation in New Brunswick 1865-66," *Canadian Historical Review* no.55, 1974

----------- *Timothy Warren Anglin 1822-1896: Irish Catholic Canadian*, University of Toronto Press, 1977

Bellot, Hugh, *Ireland and Canada: Studies in Comparative Constitutional Law and Politics*, Reeves and Turner, London, 1893

Berger, Carl (ed.), *Imperial Relations in the Age of Laurier*, University of Toronto Press, 1969

------------ *The Sense of Power: Studies in the Ideas of Canadian Imperialism, 1867-1914*, University of Toronto Press, 1970

Blake, Edward, *The Irish Question, with Special Reference to Home Rule in Canada*, London, 1892

Bovey, W., "This Democratic Empire," *Empire Club Speeches*, Toronto, 1940

Boyle, John W., "A Fenian Protestant in Canada: Robert Lindsay Crawford, 1910-22," *Canadian Historical Review* 52:2, June 1971

Brady, Alexander, "The New Dominion," *Canadian Historical Review* 4, 1923

---------------- *Thomas D'Arcy McGee*, MacMillan of Canada, Toronto, 1925

Bray, Matthew, "'Fighting as an Ally': The English-Canadian Patriotic Response to the Great War," *Canadian Historical Review* LXI, 2, 1980

Brown, Robert; Cook, Ramsay, *Canada, 1896-1921: A Nation Transformed*, McClelland and Stewart, Toronto, 1974

Burns, R.B., "D'Arcy McGee and the Fenians," M. Harmon, ed., *Fenians and Fenianism*, University of Washington Press, Seattle, 1970

----------- "D'Arcy McGee and the Fenians: A Study of the Interaction Between Irish Nationalism and the American Environment," *University Review*, Dublin, 1967

----------- "Who Shall Separate Us? The Montreal Irish and the Great War," *The Untold Story: The Irish in Canada*, (Robert O'Driscoll and Lorna Reynolds, eds.), Celtic Arts of Canada, Toronto, 1988

Cleland, Rev. William, *History Of The Presbyterian Church In Ireland, For Readers On This Side Of The Atlantic*, Hart and Company, Toronto, 1890

Conner, D.G., The Irish-Canadian Image and Self-Image, 1840-1870, MA Dissertation, University of British Columbia, 1976

Conway, S., Upper Canadian Orangeism in the 19th Century: Aspects of a Pattern of Disruption, MA Thesis, Queens, Kingston, 1977

Cottrell, Michael, "Irish Catholic Politics in Ontario," *The Untold Story: The Irish in Canada*

----------------------- "St. Patrick's Day Parades in Nineteenth-Century Toronto: A Study of Immigrant Adjustment and Elite Control," *Histoire Sociale* May 1992

Cross, D.S., *The Irish in Montreal, 1867-1896*, MA, McGill, Montreal, 1969

Currie, Philip, "Reluctant Britons: Toronto's Irish Community, Home Rule, and the Great War," *Ontario History*, March 1995

---------------- "Toronto Orangeism and the Irish Question, 1911-16," *Ontario History*, December 1995

Davis, H.A., "The Fenian Raid on New Brunswick," *Canadian Historical Review* 36, 1955

Davis, Richard, "Irish Nationalism in Manitoba, 1870-1922," *The Untold Story: The Irish in Canada*

Doherty, E.J., An Analysis of the Social and Political Thought in the Irish Canadian Press in Upper Canada, 1858-1867, MA Thesis, University of Waterloo, 1977

Galvin, Martin, "The Jubilee Riots in Toronto," *Annual Reports*, Canadian Catholic Historical Association, Ottawa, 1959

Gowan, Mark, "'To Share in the Burdens of Empire': Toronto's Catholics and the Great War, 1914-1918," *Catholics at the 'Gathering Place': Historical Essays on the Archdiocese of Toronto, 1841-1891*, Canadian Catholic Historical Association, Toronto, 1993

------------ "The De-Greening of the Irish: Toronto's Irish Catholic Press, Imperialism, and the Forging of a New Identity, 1887-1914," *Historical Papers*, Canadian Catholic Historical Association, Ottawa, 1989

Grannan, R.C., "Thomas D'Arcy McGee and Confederation in the Maritimes," *Canadian Catholic Historical Association Reports* 20, 1953

Hansard, House of Commons Debates, Ottawa (1882-1922; 1937-1949)

Harkness, D.W., "Mr. de Valera's Dominion: Irish Relations with Britain and the Commonwealth, 1932-38," *Journal of Commonwealth Political Studies*, November 1970

-------------- *The Restless Dominion: The Irish Free State and the British Commonwealth of Nations, 1921-31*, London, 1969

Haultain, Arnold, *A Selection from Goldwin Smith's Correspondence Comprising Letters Chiefly to and from his English Friends, Between the Years 1846 and 1910*, McClelland and Goodchild, Toronto, 1913

----------------, *Reminiscences by Goldwin Smith*, Macmillan, New York, 1910

Hogan, Brian, "The Guelph Novitiate Raid: Conscription, Censorship and Bigotry During the Great War," *Historical Papers*, Canadian Catholic Historical Association, Ottawa, 1978

------------ "The Second World War and the Saga of the Irish Regiment of Canada," *The Untold Story: The Irish in Canada*

Horall, S.W., Canada and the Irish Question: A Study of the Canadian Response to Irish Home Rule 1882-1893, MA Thesis, Carleton University, 1966

Houston, C.J.; Smyth, W.J., *Irish Emigration and Canadian Settlement: Patterns, Links, and Letters*, University of Toronto Press, 1990

------------------------------ *The Sash Canada Wore: A Historical Geography of the Orange Order in Canada*, University of Toronto Press, 1980

------------------------------ "Transferred Loyalties: Orangeism in the United States and Ontario," *American Review of Canadian Studies* 14:2, 1984

Johnston, A., "Popery and Progress: Anti-Catholicism in Mid-Nineteenth Century Nova Scotia," *Dalhousie Review* 64:1, 1984

Kealey, G.S., "Orangemen and the Corporation," in Victor Russell, ed., *Forging a Consensus: Historical Essays on Toronto*, University of Toronto Press, Toronto, 1984

Kenny, John, *The Road to Hillsborough: The Shaping of the Anglo-Irish Agreement*, Pergamon Press, New York, 1986

Lipset, Seymour, *Continental Divide*, Routledge, Chapman and Hall Inc., 1990

Lynch, Bryan, *The Ulster Loyalists*, Toronto, 1886

Lyne, D.C., "Irish-Canadian Financial Contributions to the Home Rule Movement in the 1890s," *Studia Hibernica* 7, 1967

----------; Toner, Peter, "Fenianism in Canada, 1874-1884," *Studia Hibernica* 12, 1974

McEvoy, Fred, "Canada, Ireland and the Commonwealth: The Declaration of the Irish Republic, 1948-9," *Irish Historical Studies*, 1983

------------- "Canadian-Irish Relations During the Second World War," *The Journal of Imperial and Commonwealth History*, January 1977

McGee, R.F., *The Reaction of the Toronto Irish Press to Fenianism and Orangeism, 1864-66*, MA Thesis, University of Ottawa, 1969

McGee, Thomas D'Arcy, *The Irish Position in British and in Republican North America*, M. Longmore & Co. Printing House, Montreal, 1866

Miller, J.R., "Anti-Catholic Thought in Victorian Canada," *Canadian Historical Review* 66, 1985

McKeown, H.C., *The Life and Labors of the Most Rev. John Joseph Lynch*, J.A. Sadlier, Toronto, 1886

Miller, K., *Emigrants and Exiles: Ireland and the Exodus to North America*, Oxford University Press, Oxford, 1985

Moir, John, "Canadian Protestant Reaction to the Ne Temere Decree," *Study Sessions* 48, Canadian Catholic Historical Association, Ottawa, 1981

Murphy, John A., "The Anglo-Irish Treaty and After: The Canadian Model and Context," *The Untold Story: The Irish in Canada*

Nelson, F.M., *The Orange Order in Canadian Politics*, MA Thesis, Queens, Kingston, 1950

Nicholson, M., "Irish Tridentine Catholicism in Victorian Toronto: Vessel for Ethno-Religious Persistence," *Historical Papers*, Canadian Catholic Historical Association, Ottawa, 1983

------------- "The Irish Experience in Ontario: Rural or Urban?," *Urban History Review* 14:1, 1985

John O'Connor, *Letters of John O'Connor, M.P. on Fenianism: addressed to His Excellency the Right*

Honourable John Young, P.C., G.C.B., G.C.MG., governor-general of Canada, Toronto, 1870

O'Hanly, J., *The Political Standing of the Irish Catholics in Canada*, Ottawa, 1872

Page, Robert, "Canada and the Imperial Idea in the Boer War Years," *Journal of Canadian Studies* 5, 1970

Parr, G., "The Welcome and the Wake, Attitudes in Canada West Toward the Irish Famine Migration," *Ontario History* LXVI, 1974

Pennefather, R.S., *The Orange and the Black*, T.H. Best Printing Company, Toronto, 1984

Perin, Roberto, *Rome in Canada: The Vatican and Canadian Affairs in the Late Victorian Age*, University of Toronto Press, Toronto, 1990

Pickersgill, J.W., *The Mackenzie King Record*, volume 1: 1939-1944, University of Toronto Press, Toronto, 1960

Prenter, Samuel, "The Religious Difficulty Under Home Rule: The Nonconformist View," *Against Home Rule: The Case For The Union* (S. Rosenbaum,ed.), Kennikat Press, London, 1970 (1912)

Raymond, R.J., "American Public Opinion and Irish Neutrality, 1939-1945," *Eire/Ireland*, Spring 1983

Reilly, Wayne G., "Political Violence in Quebec and Northern Ireland," *British Journal of Canadian Studies* 10:1, 1995

Schull, Edward, *Edward Blake: The Man of the Other Way (1833-1881)*, Macmillan of Canada, Toronto, 1975

--------------- *Edward Blake: Leader and Exile (1881-1912)*, Macmillan of Canada, Toronto, 1976

Shanahan, David, *Irish Catholic Journalists and the New Nationality in Canada, 1857-1870*, MA Thesis, Lakehead University, 1984

Saunders, Leslie, *The Story of Orangeism*, Toronto, 1941

Senior, Hereward, "Orangeism in Ontario Politics, 1872-1896," in Donald Swainson, ed., *Oliver Mowat's Ontario*, Macmillan of Canada, Toronto, 1972

----------------- *Orangeism: The Canadian Phase*, McGraw-Hill, Toronto, 1973

----------------- "Quebec and the Fenians," *Canadian Historical Review* 48, 1967

----------------- *The Fenians and Canada*, Macmillan, Toronto, 1978

Siegfried, Andre, *The Race Question in Canada*, Nash, London, 1907

Skelton, O.D., *Life and Letters of Sir Wilfrid Laurier*, Oxford University Press, Toronto, 1921

Smith, Goldwin, Irish History and Irish Character, J.H. and James Parker, Oxford and London, 1862

-------------- Dismemberment No Remedy, London, 1886

Snell, J.G., "Thomas D'Arcy McGee and the American Republic," *Canadian Review of American Studies* 3:1, 1972

Stacey, C.P., "A Fenian Interlude: The Story of Michael Murphy," *Canadian Historical Review* 15, 1934

----------- *Arms, Men and Governments: The War Policies of Canada 1939-1945*, Ottawa 1970

----------   "Fenianism and the Rise of National Feeling in Canada at the Time of Confederation," *Canadian Historical Review* 12, 1931

Stamp, Robert, "Empire Day in the Schools of Ontario: The Training of Young Imperialists," *Journal of Canadian Studies*, 1973

Stortz, G., "The Catholic Church and Irish Nationalism in Toronto, 1850-1900," *The Untold Story: The Irish in Canada*

----------   "The Irish Catholic Press in Toronto, 1887-1892: The Years of Transition," *Journal of Canadian Studies* 10:3, 1984

Strahan, J.A., "The Position and Prospects of Ulster," *Dalhousie Review* 1925

Tarr, E.J., "What Next in Ireland," *Empire Club Speeches* 4 November 1937

Thompson, J.H.; Seager, Allen, Canada 1922-1939: Decades of Discord, McClelland and Stewart Ltd., Toronto, 1990 (1985)

Toner, P.M., "'The Green Ghost': Canada's Fenians and the Raids," *Eire/Ireland* 16:4, 1981

----------   "The Home Rule League in Canada: Fortune, Fenians and Failure," *Canadian Journal of Irish Studies*, vol.15, July 1989

Watt, J.T., "Anti-Catholic Nativism in Canada: The Protestant Protective Association," *Canadian Historical Review* 48, 1967

Wigley, Philip G., *Canada and the Transition to Commonwealth: British-Canadian Relations, 1917-1926*, Cambridge University Press, 1977

Wilson, Andrew, *Irish-America and the Ulster Conflict, 1968-1995*, Catholic University of America Press, Washington D.C., 1995

Newspapers and Magazines

Calgary Herald
Canadian Churchman
Canada Presbyterian
Canadian Baptist
Canadian Freeman
Catholic New Times
Catholic Register
Catholic Record
Celtic Connection
Charlottetown Examiner
Christian Guardian
Edmonton Journal
Evening Telegram
Globe and Mail
Guelph Evening Mercury
Halifax Herald
Hamilton Spectator
Irish Canadian
Kingston British Whig
London Free Press
London Times
Macleans
Mail and Empire
Manitoba/Winnipeg Free Press
Montreal Daily Star
Montreal Gazette
Nanaimo Free Press
Orange Sentinel
Ottawa Citizen
Presbyterian Record
Presbyterian Witness (Halifax)
Presbyterian Witness (Toronto)
Regina Morning Leader
Saskatoon Star-Phoenix
The Week
The Bystander
The Statesman
Toronto Daily Star
Toronto Globe
Toronto World

United Church Observer
Vancouver Daily World
Vancouver Province
Victoria Daily Colonist
Victoria Daily Times